MAKING
BLACK GIRLS
COUNT IN
MATH EDUCATION

MAKING BLACK GIRLS COUNT IN MATH EDUCATION

A BLACK FEMINIST VISION FOR TRANSFORMATIVE TEACHING

NICOLE M. JOSEPH

HARVARD EDUCATION PRESS
CAMBRIDGE, MA

Paperback ISBN 978-1-68253-774-9

Library of Congress Cataloging-in-Publication Data is on file.

Published by Harvard Education Press,
an imprint of the Harvard Education Publishing Group
Harvard Education Press
8 Story Street
Cambridge, MA 02138

Cover Design: Patrick Ciano
Cover Image: Klaus Vedfelt/DigitalVision via Getty Images

The typefaces in this book are Myriad Pro and Scala

CONTENTS

SERIES FOREWORD

When I was in graduate school, my grandmother (who was not formally educated and lived to be ninety-two years old) would often ask me about the work I was doing. Excited to share, I would talk with her about the demanding challenges I faced in my work. I talked about nonsensical policies that seemed to perpetuate and maintain the status quo. I would tell her about the funding challenges faced by young people from particular communities. I would share my frustration that high school students were working part-time jobs to support their families and still expected to "produce" the same outputs as those who did not have to work. I talked about how inequitable, unfair, unjust, and alarming situations were (and are) in society and education. And after I finished sharing my analyses and critiques with her, my grandmother would intently stare at me, looking firmly in my eyes, and simply say, "Keep pressing!"

Making Black Girls Count in Math Education is a groundbreaking intersectional project, inundated with transformative stories about, from, and with Black girls and women about their mathematical thinking, development, learning, and outcomes. Joseph amplifies what is and should be possible when mechanisms are in place to co-construct with Black girls and women humanizing, relevant, and responsive educational ecological systems. What Joseph has produced in *Making Black Girls Count in Math Education* is an intellectually stimulating, historically grounded, forward-thinking, accessibly written book that will make a difference in the fields of mathematics, education, and mathematics education. In short, *Making Black Girls Count in Math Education* addresses so many challenges Black girls and women face as they learn mathematics and simultaneously reminds readers, as my grandmother did, to keep pressing!

Grounded in theory and research, this is a beautifully written book with important implications for praxis. Rather than simply identifying, describing, and critiquing institutional structures and systems that perpetuate an inequitable status quo for Black girls and women, Joseph describes what is necessary to change—to transform and improve—the educational landscape for Black girls and women in math. Indeed, this book shows us that Black girls and women are geniuses. They are the backbone and the heartbeat of families, communities, and educational spaces. However, traditional notions about what it means to learn and know mathematics lead too many Black girls and women to believe they may be incapable of succeeding in math. What Joseph shows in this book, which every single educator, community member, parent, family member, and policy maker should read, is that the success of Black girls and women in math is intricately, necessarily, and inextricably connected to their identity. In this way, mathematical and identity work must be connected. Although this is a book for many, I am especially excited for the research community to read it. Indeed, if there were ever a time when math education researchers needed to read a book and if there were ever a book that they needed to read, the time is now, and this is the book!

The narratives in this book showcase why focusing on teaching and learning mathematics alone as a subject matter is insufficient. Studying and advancing knowledge about mathematics and Black girls and women require deep cultural understandings about the ways in which racism and sexism intersect to consistently underserve and undermine these communities.

This book "talks back" to deficit notions about Black girls and women, blaming these communities for challenges they face in a mathematical maze designed to change people rather than change policies and practices. Joseph demonstrates with power and precision how traditional educational systems were not designed for Black girls and women. Still, we learn in this book about the brilliance, resilience, and fortitude of the "Mag5"—women who navigated and negotiated some of the most horrific times in our nation's history. Although Joseph identifies five Black exceptional women mathematicians, having earned their degrees from prestigious institutions of higher education during Jim Crow, we know there were many others. Thus, these stories are essential exemplars that showcase varying levels—from micro to meso to macro—of what it means to study and understand math, identity, teaching, and learning. Moreover, through careful, astute, and deliberate units of analysis, Joseph demonstrates how, in her words, that *"Jim Crow represented the legitimization of anti-Black racism."* However, even amid oppression, the Mag5 kept pressing.

Joseph tackles some of the most relevant issues facing Black girls and women. She shepherds readers into what it takes to construct and cultivate joyful, humanizing, opportunity-centered spaces where young people and adults are able to be and practice their full authentic selves in, through, and for mathematics. The book is importantly deep and yet broad. For instance, Joseph addresses issues of segregation and desegregation. She discusses the role and salience of white supremacy. She uncovers the ways in which whiteness as well as white and male privilege manifest in policies and practices. Joseph explains how anti-Blackness as a never-ending vehicle is organized and orchestrated to maintain whiteness. Joseph implores us to define and name inequity and provides tools for readers on how to disrupt injustice. Amplifying Black girls' voices, this book is about curriculum, pedagogy, critical consciousness, and cultivating "robust mathematical identities" with Black girls and women. Joseph's work is an essential model for sustaining Black girls' mathematical identity and joy. Ultimately, Joseph implicitly encourages readers to keep pressing.

In conclusion, Joseph has produced a game-changing book that reminds me of the words my grandmother shared with me many years ago. I suspect those words may feel under-nuanced, too simplistic, or perhaps even unthinkable during these times of unprecedented challenges.

Certainly, the work of justice and equity is not easy and will likely only get more challenging over the coming years. Yet, this book represents a collective call that we must—on behalf of and in support of Black girls and women—*keep pressing!*

—H. Richard Milner IV
Author, *Start Where You Are But Don't Stay There*
Cornelius Vanderbilt Chair of Education, Vanderbilt University

FOREWORD

What does it take for a nation to fulfill the full promise of the mathematical talent of its citizenry? Nicole Joseph has crafted this volume to underscore both the travails and opportunities that Black women and girls face in their pursuit of mathematics. While so much of the discourse around mathematics and African Americans has been shaded with the language of deficit, rather than potential—and these deficit perspectives permeate all aspects of mathematics teaching and learning in the United States, Joseph argues—Joseph and others exploring the power of Black women in mathematics are painting a more complete picture. With *#BlackGirlMagic* and *#StrongBlackWomen* prominent in the social media discourse, we are reminded that these phrases may not capture fully what often must be an incredible combination of talent and hard work in the face of odds and obstacles that few others must experience. In chapters exploring key issues in mathematics classrooms at all levels (e.g., curriculum, pedagogy, assessment) as well as the broader context of teacher education and practice, politics, and policy influencing mathematics education, Joseph carefully documents, describes, and analyzes the mathematical worlds of Black girls and women.

This important volume does more than broaden narratives about mathematics in the United States. It illuminates important theoretical perspectives related to racism and sexism in the sciences and provides a road map to leveraging Black women's mathematical creativity, strength, leadership, advocacy, and perseverance. Asked once to summarize her accomplishments, Evelyn Boyd Granville, the third Black woman to obtain her PhD in mathematics, stated: "First of all, showing that women can do mathematics." Then she added, "Being an African-American woman, letting people know we have brains too."[1] Granville and her counterparts demonstrated excellence and did so in an era in the United States of race-based and gender-based stratification that suggested that women were incapable of scientific pursuits and, further, that sought to relegate Black women to manual labor. Granville's quote—a familiar one to many Black women mathematicians—illustrates what has been called the "double bind" of being both a woman and a Black person in mathematics. The uniqueness of this status—and its attendant social and cultural contexts within and beyond the field of mathematics—has long deserved a clear-eyed and careful examination, which Joseph eloquently and compellingly provides in these pages.

Drawing from critical race theory and Black feminist perspectives, Joseph uses a deeply grounded approach to explore the mathematical lives of Black girls and women along the P–20 pipeline. Too often in social science work, a common trope persists: "All the women are White, and all the Black people are men." Attending to the important social, cultural, and political intersections of the spaces and places that Black women and girls occupy, as well as important historical and contemporary issues that uniquely apply to them, this work contributes to deeper analyses of the educational and professional opportunities and experiences of Black girls and women in service to enhancing education and life outcomes.

The excellence of Black women in mathematics is seen in the stories of Black women mathematicians, who, often without credit or recognition, labor in service to a broader ideal of ensuring that more people excluded from mathematics gain access to the field and contribute to its development, as I have written elsewhere.[2] But, as Joseph writes, it is important to count the costs of "what has been lost." There are many examples of Black women's mathematical skills and interests, stunted in terms of access to formal mathematics learning environments, but exhibited in other areas of American life (the Black women quilters of Gee's Bend come to mind, with their intricate, complex geometries). There are so many stories of *invisible* Black women mathematical geniuses, told by family members and colleagues, who may never be widely known. The most widely known example of a previously *invisible* Black woman in mathematics may be Katherine Johnson of *Hidden Figures* fame. Elsewhere I have spoken and written about Johnson and how, in the last decade of her life, she rightfully received great attention for her and her Black women colleagues' contributions to NASA and its earlier incarnations. But it is important to remember that Johnson's life was not in reality a Hollywood film. She was a real person, for whom racism and sexism operated in ways to obstruct her education and career paths. It is a testament to her and to the Black community that supported her that she was able to surmount these obstacles, but still a terrible commentary that she had to work against these obstacles, supported by only her family and her community for many years. Where would the space program be now if Katherine Johnson and others like her had been allowed to flourish to their full potential; if Johnson had been able to pursue graduate studies (including a doctorate in mathematics, if she wanted one) unfettered by racism and sexism? When Joseph delineates the structures and practices that thwart Black girls' and women's opportunities in mathematics, it is not to point out explanations for so-called achievement gaps, but rather to highlight that these structures and practices are detrimental to not just Black women and girls, but to all of us who are losing out on their brilliance and contributions to the field. Why should Black women and girls have to work harder than others to persist and thrive in mathematics? These additional gauntlets are real measures of continued obstruction, painted as color-blind, but in reality, highly colored by lingering and dominating racist and sexist policies and practices.

We must be grateful for Joseph's vision and tenacity for this research and her efforts to craft welcoming and inclusive mathematical worlds for Black girls and women. Throughout this volume, she highlights that Black women and girls—historically and in contemporary times—have advocated, agitated for, and created better mathematical worlds where their full humanity, potential, and excellence is seen, encouraged, and rewarded. Black girls and women should not have to be alone in this quest, and they should not have to rely on serendipity of opportunity to study with or work with well-intentioned individuals. These systemic issues require systemic solutions. Joseph has provided a detailed and informative framework for us all to do the work of reimagining mathematics as a fully inclusive, welcoming, and rewarding field of play, study, and research.

—Erica N. Walker
Clifford Brewster Upton Professor of Mathematical Education
Teachers College, Columbia University

PREFACE

I remember being in Ms. Elorante's third-grade class at Benjamin Franklin Day Elementary School in Seattle, Washington. Ms. Elorante was an older white woman, thin, with cottony white hair. One day we were doing math, and I raised my hand to answer a question, but she did not call on me. Unbeknown to me, my mother was standing outside the door observing our class, and she saw my "little Black hand" (Mom's words) waving to get Ms. Elorante's attention so that I could answer the math question. When class was over, Mom walked into the room and asked Ms. Elorante why she did not call on me to answer the question. Ms. Elorante looked a little confused, flushed, and said that she did not see my hand. Mom told her, "Nicole will be removed from this class today"; Mom felt that Ms. Elorante was racist. I do not know if Ms. Elorante was racist or not—I was only eight years old—but my mother saw that I was being ignored and perhaps treated unfairly and differently. Because I was moved into an "advanced" third-grade class the following few days, a class that opened my potential and changed my mathematics trajectory, I experienced what it felt like to have someone advocate on my behalf. While I did not have the words to name this phenomenon, I experienced it in my heart and my spirit, and I felt sanguine.

From that point on, my life would never be the same. I excelled like crazy in mathematics—I learned how to do school mathematics—and became the quintessential Black girl in middle and high school who represented what it meant to be academically successful. An undergraduate degree in economics and minor in mathematics set me on the path to becoming a secondary mathematics teacher, as the state of Washington

certified me to teach preK–12 and later coach several mathematics teachers (mainly white males). But deep inside I felt something was wrong
because none of my friends in middle and high school and college were
in the higher-level mathematics courses with me, and I was usually the
only Black girl. At first it was cute, and I liked being the only one, but
quickly, I begin to question why I was the only one? At the young age of
seventeen, questions about equity in mathematics for Black girls began
to emerge. Two decades later, as a professor of mathematics education,
I am not only asking these questions, but working both independently
and in collaboration and solidarity with Black girls, researchers, parents,
teachers, and others who are genuinely concerned about supporting Black
girls' mathematics learning and development to answer these questions.
I remember my third-grade experience with Ms. Elorante as if it happened yesterday. I share it because it is a vivid reminder to me about my
purpose—that Black girls matter and must be protected, nurtured, and
advocated for in schools and in mathematics education.

INTRODUCTION

Making Black Girls Count in Math Education is a meta-synthesis of ten years of research and scholarship examining issues related to Black girls, their intersectional identities, and mathematics.[1] Such a text and scope are needed because Black girls matter and must be protected, nurtured, and advocated for in mathematics education. But a significant impediment to this work of advocacy is that we do not deeply understand— research, practice, and policy—the issues of principle facing Black girls in mathematics contexts and how to eliminate them. We do not understand the issues they face in mathematics because education researchers rarely design and publish studies that center Black girls as subject, not object, meaning Black girls are seldom knowledge producers and authors of their own narratives about their mathematics experiences. And because we have not focused on Black girl stories in mathematics education research, our theorization about the multifaceted and complex realities Black girls face in their mathematics education trajectories is limited.

In addition to the scholarly neglect, we also do not understand issues facing Black girls in mathematics contexts because researchers often use single-axis analysis; they treat race, gender, and other socially constructed identities as mutually exclusive categories of experience.[2] Black girls are multidimensional, and their lived experiences in mathematics must be understood through intersectionality or other critical intersectional frameworks.[3] Consequently, *Making Black Girls Count in Math Education* disrupts uncritical and essentialist thinking about Black girls' and women's mathematics education in US society. Much is lost, devalued, and erased when we do not politicize Black girls' mathematics access, learning, development, participation, and achievement. Parallel with this critical analysis is the work of coalition building, so I hope to not only challenge, but be a bridge builder and inspirer to my peers and the world for anyone who desires to engage in what Paulo Freire calls praxis work.[4]

My hope is that *Making Black Girls Count in Math Education* becomes a useful intersectional project that contributes to transforming our knowledge of Black girls and women in the US mathematics education system. I invite Black girls, their families, teachers, academic administrators, curriculum developers, grant makers, policy makers, and other stakeholders to first listen, reflect, ask questions, and then do something (praxis) about changing the life conditions of Black girls, whereby they deeply understand that they can master mathematics and know themselves as critically and creatively conscious scholars, educators, and activists. This introduction begins by highlighting important current Black girl initiatives and their contributions in conversation with this book's vision. Next, I historicize Black girls' and women's experiences in mathematics by uplifting and rendering narratives of the first five Black women to earn doctorates in mathematics, known by my nomenclature as the Magnificent Five. Using a historical context to unpack Black girls' and women's mathematics experiences sets up the reader for why and how critical frameworks and methodologies ground *Making Black Girls Count in Math Education*. I close the introduction with chapter summaries and takeaways.

THE BLACK GIRL MOVEMENT IN US CONTEXTS

A national movement in the United States that emphasizes the importance of Black girls' lives and the confluence of social media, federal attention, and research funding is driving the increased visibility. Examples include #BlackGirlMagic, the social media campaign about increasing positive self-identity of Black girls and women that went viral in 2013; the NoVo Foundation's announcement of the largest commitment ever made ($90 million dollars) by a private foundation to address the structural inequalities facing girls and young women of color in the United States in 2016; the White House Council on Women and Girls commitments of $118 million from various women's foundations and academic institutions across the country to improve the lives of young women of color through new programs and research; and the most recent campaign, #1billion4Blackgirls.[5]

On September 15, 2020, the fifty-seventh anniversary of the 1963 Birmingham, Alabama, church bombing that killed four Black girls, a group of prominent Black women launched the Black Girl Freedom Fund.[6] They wrote an open letter pointing out that while Black Lives Matter attracts strong philanthropic support, "Black girls and young women still remain adultified, victimized by violence, and erased from the very same social justice movement for which they continue to risk their lives."[7] These national efforts—spanning the public and private sectors and academe—are important because they acknowledge race, racism, sexism, and other structural inequalities. However, none are addressing the underrepresentation, underperformance, and retention of Black girls and women in mathematics, which is a phenomenon inextricably connected to issues of *race, racism, and sexism* and other intersectional oppressions.[8] Black girls experience intellectual violence, adultification, and erasure in mathematics contexts. *Making Black Girls Count in Math Education* takes up this agenda by unapologetically identifying and discussing issues Black girls face in the US mathematics education system—from dehumanizing learning spaces to decontextualized curriculum and gendered anti-Black mathematics education policies. But I do not stay there—this book reimagines and provides a vision for what is possible when Black girls have limitless possibilities in mathematics.

HISTORICIZING LEARNING (MATHEMATICS) WHILE BLACK GIRLS

Mathematics contexts are full of signals that Black girls do not belong. Some signals across the pipeline can include tracking her into the low-level mathematics classroom, focusing on her behavior rather than her mathematics development, peers not viewing her as a contributor in class, teachers not teaching her, students questioning her mathematics abilities, university faculty telling her that she should have learned this or that in high school, or not being asked to be on research projects to teach or publish. This is a harmful myth, because Black girls do belong in mathematics, and we have been here all along, but often hidden in plain sight (chapter 1 introduces a typology of the invisibility of Black girls and women in mathematics).

That Black girls and women are hidden in plain sight in mathematics contexts suggests something about the discipline and culture of mathematics. Some scholars have characterized mathematics as a white, patriarchal space unsupportive of Black girls and women whereby Black girls and women experience tensions.[9] Mathematics as a white, patriarchal space is historically exclusionary, and not new. Black people, and Black girls especially in the South during the late nineteenth and early twentieth centuries, were discouraged from pursuing any professional training outside of the ministry or teaching.[10] The discouragement was complete because whites, both by precept and practice, treated the *professions* (i.e., doctors, attorneys, engineers) as "aristocratic spheres to which Negroes should not aspire."[11] Consequently, many Blacks became complicit, having learned from their oppressors "to say to their children that there were certain spheres into which they should not go because they would have no chance therein for development."[12] Black students, and Black girls specifically, are still implicitly and explicitly dissuaded from studying certain subjects, such as mathematics. The social and cultural norms, ideologies, and structures of mathematics often prevent Black girls and women from viewing themselves as mathematics community insiders.[13]

But when we look at history, we find examples of Black women who "talked back" to the social and cultural norms, ideologies, and structures of mathematics to forge careers as mathematicians.[14] Drs. Euphemia Haynes, Evelyn Boyd Granville, Marjorie Lee Brown, Gloria Conyers Hewitt, and Vivienne Malone-Mayes (hereafter the Magnificent Five or Mag5) completed doctorates in pure mathematics in the years 1943, 1949, 1950, 1962, and 1966, respectively, at Catholic University; Yale University; the University of Michigan; the University of Washington, Seattle; and the University of Texas, Austin. These women were working toward doctorates in mathematics during Jim Crow, an era in American history that should have silenced them completely. Jim Crow was the name of the racial caste system that operated primarily in Southern states between 1877 and the mid-1960s. It was a series of rigid anti-Black laws in which most African Americans were relegated to the status of second-class citizens. *Jim Crow represented the legitimization of anti-Black racism.* Situating the Mag5's mathematics narratives within this geopolitical context is important because it illuminates texture and nuance about what makes Black girls' and women's mathematics development and experiences unique. Their stories bring to the fore how Black women experienced isolation, vulnerability, resistance, resilience, and interlocking systems of oppression.

The Mag5 attended Historically Black Colleges and Universities (HBCUs) and women's colleges for their undergraduate degrees. Close readings and analysis of the Mag5's archived biographies suggest that they valued these segregated experiences for many reasons, including the presence of role models and teachers who had unequivocal faith in their abilities to become anything they desired, including a mathematician. Teachers at HBCUs were mostly Black and educated, and many of these instructors saw their mission as educating Black students to their highest potential so that they could become whatever they wanted and make positive contributions to society and their communities.[15]

This notion of Black teachers teaching in the South for Black excellence is evidenced in author Margot Lee Shetterly's narrative, *Hidden Figures.* She described her hometown of Hampton, Virginia, as a place where she "knew so many African Americans working in science, math, and engineering that [she] thought that's just what Black folks did."[16] She writes that the "face of science was brown like mine."[17] Five of Shetterly's father's seven siblings were engineers, her next-door neighbor taught physics at Hampton University, and even her church "abounded with mathematicians."[18] Shetterly revealed that in 1945, NASA employed twenty-five Black women as human "computers" or mathematicians, because they coaxed numbers out of calculators on a twenty-four-hour schedule. Although there was representation and role models at NASA, these women were held back in terms of advancement, promotion, pay, and recognition. The Mag5 also experienced limitations. All were faculty members at some point in their careers, but they were not encouraged to publish their work in academic journals. Since most had close connections to their families and communities and believed in educational equity in mathematics, they mainly served their communities in significant ways, including as mathematics teachers and curriculum experts.

The intersectional complexities of the Mag5's lived experiences as mathematicians are distinct, because, on the one hand, they were a part of a vanguard—it is difficult for anyone to earn a doctorate in pure mathematics—yet they were also outsiders to the larger mathematics community in that their peers did not view them as authorities in the field.[19] This was probably because the Mag5 seldom published in academic and research journals where editors more than likely exercised discriminatory practices.[20] Additionally, while they contributed to their own communities, they may have aspired to do more in the research field. But Black women and girls must think through the intersectional tensions: "Do I want to potentially fragment my identities to be in the company of individuals who don't even think I belong in the space (race or gender or race/gender) so my intellectual work and labor is about proving myself, or do I want to live an authentic life in service of my humanity and mental health?"[21] These are questions that many white women and Black men in mathematics seldom must ask themselves. Thus, *Making Black Girls Count in Math Education* invokes criticality using intersectional frames and methodologies to expose how mainstream mathematics culture and communities create norms, expectations, pathways, and profiles of who they deem a real mathematician, and how these discourses exclude Black girls and women.

INTERSECTIONAL ANALYSES: MAKING THE SEEMINGLY MUNDANE BEAR WEIGHT

Although their numbers are few (see statistics in chapter 2), Black girls and women do persist in mathematics to the doctorate degree, and they experience isolation, vulnerability, and invisibility. They also resile by using resistance strategies in mathematics contexts.[22] Naturally, their pathways to the mathematics doctorate are varied, as Erica Walker points out in her seminal text, *Beyond Banneker: Black Mathematicians and the Paths to Excellence*.[23] However, their paths are alike in that racism, sexism, and other systems of oppression assault them all along their road to becoming mathematicians. Racism and sexism are social oppressions that have historical roots and contemporary consequences, and they contribute to the underrepresentation and underperformance of Black girls and women in mathematics.

Making Black Girls Count in Math Education uses intersectional analyses and methods to make visible both the problems and the promises Black girls and women face in mathematics and mathematics education. By *intersectional analysis,* I mean that I use critical intersectional frameworks, such as critical race theory, Cynthia Dillard's endarkened feminist epistemology (EFE), and Tamara Butler's Black girl cartography to illuminate the experiences of Black women and girls in mathematics in six topic areas—learning spaces, curriculum, pedagogy, assessment, teacher education, and policy—to show complex connections between Black girls' learning mathematics and larger interlocking systems of oppression.[24] I also employ Chayla Haynes et al.'s intersectionality methodology (IM).[25] In each chapter, I invoke these different critical frameworks and methodologies, not at the same time, but when deemed appropriate for advancing complex arguments about the Black girls and women and their mathematics learning and development in US contexts.

Critical Race Theory

Critical race theory (CRT) advances a strategy to foreground and account for the role of race and racism in education and works toward the elimination of racism as part of a broader goal of dismantling other forms of subordination based on gender, class, sexuality, language, and national origin. CRT in education is a set of foundational insights, perspectives, methods, and pedagogies that seek to identify, analyze, and transform those structural and cultural aspects of education that maintain dominant racial positions in and out of the classroom.[26] CRT has several tenets, and I discuss a few of them next.

CRT scholars posit that racism is an everyday occurrence in American society and its institutions. Black girls and women comprise about 6 percent of the US population, and they live as racialized beings, particularly in schools.[27] Because race and racism are entrenched constructs in American life, this book deconstructs and disrupts ideas of meritocracy, colorblindness, neutrality, and objectivity. CRT validates the idea that mathematics spaces are not neutral because learning mathematics is a complex notion for Black people.[28] Nothing about the spaces or contexts in which Black girls and women learn mathematics is neutral or objective.[29] Black women and girls are often the only representatives of their race in advanced mathematics courses and graduate programs; they must constantly prove their worth and value to the mathematics community while enduring isolation, hyper-visibility, invisibility, microaggressions, and other negative experiences.[30]

CRT in education rejects ahistoricism and examines the historical linkages between contemporary educational inequity and historical patterns of racial oppression. One way of engaging in this work is through counternarratives.[31] Danny Martin has written extensively about sociohistorical, community, school, and intrapersonal forces contributing to resilience and success in mathematics, but that work has not focused on Black girls and women explicitly.[32] Counternarratives of Black girls' and women's achievement in mathematics disrupt normative discourse about their underachievement and unpreparedness. CRT also elevates the importance of praxis based on the notion that researchers should be working toward social justice (i.e., the elimination of racism and sexism) and the empowerment of people of color and other subordinated groups in our society.[33] In addressing the issues related to underrepresentation and underperformance of Black girls and women in mathematics, understanding theory is important but not sufficient. *Making Black Girls Count in Math Education* pushes for a transformative policy agenda that is rooted in intersectional theory, reflection, and action in service of the commitment to affirmation of Black girls' humanity and well-being.[34]

Endarkened Feminist Epistemology

Endarkened feminist epistemology (EFE) articulates how reality is known when based in the historical roots of Black feminist thought, embodying a distinguishable difference in cultural standpoint, located in the intersection and overlap of the culturally constructed socialization of race, gender, and other identities and the historical and contemporary contexts of oppressions and resistance for African American women.[35] Because language has historically served and continues to serve as a powerful tool in the mental, spiritual, and intellectual colonization of African Americans,

EFE allows me to use language that more accurately organizes, resists, and transforms oppressive descriptions of sociocultural phenomena and relationships. The following tweet from Dr. Terri Watson illustrates what I mean:

Black girls are *not loud*—they *want to be heard.*
Black girls are *not seeking attention*—they are *seeking a connection.*
Black girls are *not aggressive*—they *know what they want.*
Black girls are *not bossy*—*they are leaders.*
Last, Black girls are not adults.[36]

Thinking through a mathematics context, mathematics teachers sometimes characterize Black girls in ways that focus on dehumanizing them or fragmenting their identities based on the internalization of stereotypes as articulated in Watson's tweet. For example, one study examined the mathematics experiences of two middle-school Black girls, Stella and Rachel, who were hardworking mathematics students, yet their teacher viewed them as unambitious because they were from families with little traditional parental support and were full of personality, loving to sing.[37] Researchers who do not seek complexities through EFE script Black girls through deficit language and discourses. This book understands that language is epistemic; thus the analyses and interpretations aim to use language that does something toward transforming dominant ways of knowing and producing knowledge.

Black Girl Cartography

Black girl cartography (BGC) includes Black girls' intersectional identities but takes it a step further to consider *location* in the intersections—the geopolitical and sociopolitical locations of Black girls in literature and in physical places and how Black girlhood is informed, reformed, or stifled.[38] *Making Black Girls Count in Math Education* maps and charts the intersectional realities Black girls face in mathematics learning environments, curriculum, pedagogies, and assessment practices; thus this text creates Black girl space for Black girls in research and literature. In the final chapter, I advance a call for scholars to create more research that answers questions such as "What might Black girls offer via an intersectional lens about how they grapple with their Black (race) girlhood (gender) as a middle schooler (age) in a geopolitical landscape, such as a mathematics class-room or school (location/place) that is rooted in anti-Blackness, racism, sexism, and classism?" It is important for Black girls to participate in the theorization process about their own experiences where these narratives are uplifted and included in the larger conversations.

Intersectionality Methodology

Intersectionality methodology (IM) is a nuanced methodological approach for taking up intersectionality in one's study of Black women in education research, and social science research broadly. I use IM in this text because this book (a) centralizes Black girls and women as the subject, not object; (b) uses a critical lens to uncover the micro- and macro-level power rela-tions found in learning environments, curricula, pedagogies, assessments, policies, and teacher education; (c) acknowledges how power informs the research process, making a positionality statement about the researcher; (d) shows that the complex identity markers of Black girls and women learning mathematics cannot be explained by one identity dimension alone; and (e) dispels the idea that Black girls and women are monolithic

Overall, it is counterproductive to explore issues of equity and social justice in mathematics and mathematics education by solely considering race, in large part because for Black girls and women, race and gender identities intersect and cannot be divorced from each other.[39] Intersec-tional frameworks point out that socially constructed categories of race and gender, for example, generate unique histories and experiences at the point of intersection.[40] Without this type of intersectional analysis, we limit ourselves as a field in sufficiently addressing the manner in which subordination, resistance, and self-actualization manifest in the lives of Black girls and women in mathematics and mathematics education. Furthermore, since mathematics is a male-dominated domain and is em-bedded in white supremacy and patriarchy, mathematics as a discipline is uniquely primed for the use of intersectional tools.[41]

The mathematics education field and American society in general must pay attention to the important issues facing Black girls and women because their ways of knowing can contribute to solving some of the most complex challenges in our world. For example, politician Stacey Abrams, along with the women in her grassroots campaign, worked to register close to 800,000 voters from the Latino, Black, and Asian communities and were also able to turn the registrations into votes, making the state of Georgia blue for the 2020 presidential election.[42] Black women have a unique standpoint on issues of intersectional oppression, and better understanding these issues represents a starting place that can raise critical questions and insights that would not arise "in thought that begins from dominant [white males in particular] group lives."[43] Diversity in thinking drives innovation, and it is important that mathematics development and the solving of complex problems be approached by using a collection of diverse people rather than a collection of individually capable people.[44] Professor Walter Secada said that if large numbers of people perceive that they are outcasts from mathematics and science, they are less likely to support critical societal investments in STEM development.[45] Therefore, American society should consider the important ways Black women and girls can contribute to our STEM society.

CHAPTER SUMMARIES

Chapter 1, "Black Girls' and Women's Typology of Invisibility in (Mathematics) Education," uses CRT and EFE to historicize Black women's and girls' invisibility in their general education experiences, from de jure segregation to integration (i.e., the 1954 *Brown v. Board of Education of Topeka, Kansas,* court case). I then use examples from this history to present a typology for Black girls' and women's invisibility in mathematics. I argue that the infrastructure of the discipline of mathematics fails Black women and girls largely because it has been socially constructed around white supremacist, anti-Blackness, and gendered racist ideas.

Chapter 2, "Mathematics Learning Environments and Black Girls: Shifting the 'Climate' Paradigm from Dehumanizing to Human Flourishing," examines what aspects of the mathematics learning environment promote and discourage learning for Black girls and women. I answer the question by first historicizing it, unpacking the ways Black girls have been left out of the conversation and made vulnerable throughout their mathematics trajectories, because these environments have been socially constructed to privilege white interests. Mathematics contexts were not necessarily designed for Black women and girls to succeed. I then reclaim the question by advancing learning designs that can realize Black girl joy.

Chapter 3, "The Cartography of Mathematics Curricula Through Black Girlhood Geographies," explores how Black girlhood is suppressed by the epistemological processes and space of mathematics curricula. The reader learns about the mainstream mathematics curricular design, adoption, and enactment processes and how this enterprise renders Black girls' liberatory mathematics education invisible. Their invisibility is through school structures and omission that implicitly and explicitly promote the perseveration of white values and interests. I close the chapter with a sample mathematics curriculum informed by EFE and demonstrate a vision for how to design mathematics curriculum that can transform personal, social, economic, and political structures for many Black girls' liberation now and over time.

Chapter 4, "Black Feminist Mathematics Pedagogies (BlackFMP): A Pedagogical Model Toward Black Girl Joy and Liberation in Mathematics Education," explores what types of pedagogies Black girls report valuing for increasing their participation, understanding of mathematical concepts or ideas, and overall development in mathematics. I use Black girls' voices from various research studies and dissertations in the literature. I also use Black girls' mathematics experiences as a starting point to examine how we might develop and use creative and humanizing pedagogies to realize their genius, excellence, and brilliance, and make it impossible for them to fail. The examination comes through the advancement of my BlackFMP model, which includes the pedagogical dimensions of critical consciousness, robust mathematical identities, social and academic integration, and ambitious mathematics instruction aiming to create and sustain Black girl joy in their mathematics education.

Chapter 5, "'Your ACT Scores Can Stop You from Going to College': Standardized Testing and the Promise of Black Girls' Advancement," discusses high-stakes testing (summative assessments) and its consequences for Black girls. I first problematize the "math for all" rhetoric through an analysis of Black girls' mathematics achievement as measured by the National Assessment of Education Progress (NAEP) scores, with a focus on major states with large Black populations (e.g., the District of Columbia, Georgia, Louisiana, Maryland, and Mississippi). I then unpack the disconnection between mathematics standards, curriculum, instruction, and assessment by using Black girl narratives about the American College Test (ACT). The chapter closes by elevating the benefits of formative assessments for "seeing" Black girls' mathematics development and achievement, an important practice mathematics teachers should use daily in supporting Black girls' development of critical metacognitive thinking. This is one of the most powerful ways to understand what Black girls know and comprehend in their math learning.

Chapter 6, "A Talk to Mathematics Teachers Who Are Ready to Go for Broke," is an extension of chapter 4, which explored inclusive pedagogies important for Black girls' mathematics learning. Chapter 6 argues that to use liberatory pedagogies, such as those identified and discussed in chapter 4, ongoing critical self-work is necessary. My argument is inspired by the late James Baldwin, who wrote a powerful speech in 1963 called "A Talk to Teachers." I use his language "go for broke" to illuminate for pre- and in-service mathematics teachers what the critical work might look like, including things such as the intentional acknowledgment of the role systemic psychosocial, symbolic, intellectual, and psychological violence play in stymieing Black girls' strong mathematics identities and transformative mathematics learning experiences. After a brief discussion of the mathematics teaching force in the United States and some of the critical issues in the national efforts for recruiting teachers of color, especially in mathematics, I lay out a three-part plan for mathematics teachers, called transformative teachers of mathematics (TToM). I argue that these three features should be present in any plan that is pursuing liberatory mathematics education for Black girls.

The conclusion, "Where Do We Go from Here? Making Black Girls Count in Mathematics and Mathematics Education," puts forth a research agenda for Black girls and women in mathematics and mathematics education. I reiterate the importance of critique of research, practice, and policy and make recommendations for moving forward in the field.

We need more contextualized studies that include structural analyses and more quantitative studies that do intersectional analyses. We need more public scholarship to reach schools, communities, and students, a campaign for Black female mathematics teachers, and further work on scaling effective programs. The US education system is full of barriers that get in the way of Black girls and women thriving authentically in mathematics because it is centered in hegemony. Nevertheless, this final chapter ends with expectation, certitude, and optimism, including a call to Black women STEM educators working together in service of Black girls' thriving in mathematics. All readers, including scholars, practitioners, and other stakeholders, should find this book informative and transformative.

1

BLACK GIRLS' AND WOMEN'S TYPOLOGY OF INVISIBILITY IN (MATHEMATICS) EDUCATION

This chapter examines Black girls' and women's invisibility in their educational experiences, from de jure segregation to desegregation and integration (i.e., the 1954 *Brown v. Board of Education of Topeka, Kansas,* court case). I use history because no robust public record of Black girls' experiences in mathematics education exists—the archives are silent. I use examples from history to frame a typology for their invisibility in mathematics.

Black girls and women are invisible.[1] Invisible in society, invisible in asset-based research, invisible in national discourse, policy, and practice. Black girls and women are also invisible in mathematics.[2] These invisibilities are socially constructed, and they occur throughout US educational history. Although US historians have rarely (if ever) taken up social histories of mathematics education for Black girls and/or women, the narrative of Black girls' invisibility in mathematics runs parallel to their general experiences in education, especially before the passing of *Brown v. Board of Education.*[3] Farah Jasmine Griffin states emphatically that Black girls have never had true voice in our culture and suggests that their narratives are missing from the archives in historical research.[4] She goes on to say:

> For the most part they [Black girls] have not left diaries, journals, and letters to collections, libraries or historical societies; written or published autobiographies do not exist, and such sources are often those of elite and exceptional Black women recollecting their childhoods; and if ordinary Black girls are present in historical literature it is via writings that record violence against them, list them as chattel, or portray them as one-dimensional stereotypes. In addition, Black girls, scholars have shown, have been reluctant to reveal themselves to interviewers and researchers for fear of being misrepresented and misinterpreted. In spite of this, perceived absences should not keep us from looking for Black girls in the archive.

Black woman historian of education Kabria Baumgartner did just that—searched for Sarah—a five-year old Black girl who was denied admission to her local elementary school that was closest to her house by the Massachusetts Supreme Judicial Court in 1850.[5] Baumgartner critiques the mainstream white historians Stephen Kendrick and Paul Kendrick, who positioned Sarah's story as a clean slate and brings to light that Sarah C. Roberts was actually a young Black girl "thrust into the legal spotlight to win equal school rights in Boston."[6] This overall invisibility can be described as *erasure* because the narrative has been presented as if Black girls and women were not there.

In her foundational study, Elizabeth Ihle described the development of elementary, vocational, high school, and college education for Black women and girls in the South from 1865 to around the 1980s.[7] What we learn from this four-part government-commissioned study, sponsored by the Women's Educational Equity Act Program, is that intersectional biases (i.e., race and gender) significantly decreased the quality of education for Black girls and women. For example, from colonial times (pre–Civil War) and Reconstruction (1860–1880) to the mid-twentieth century, the purpose of Black girls' and women's education, especially in the South, was to improve morals and prepare for "appropriate" work.[8] Black girls and women were not to think for themselves, stand up for their ideas, or be inquisitive—all important characteristics of self-actualization and a mathematician.[9] In the next section, I describe the kind of education available to Black girls and women during this period and give examples for naming their invisibility.

LEARNING FOUNDATIONS: BLACK GIRLS' AND WOMEN'S INVISIBILITY BY SCHOOL STRUCTURES AND FAMILY INTERNALIZED OPPRESSION

Because the laws in a number of Southern states forbade the teaching of Blacks to read and write, illiteracy was rampant among newly freed slaves immediately after the Civil War (1861–1865), and therefore many Black people lacked even an elementary education.[10] Basic literacy quickly became a postwar necessity, so several mission society and Freedmen's Bureau schools were founded in the South to help Black women and men get a basic education.[11] Estimates indicate that the bureau taught some 250,000 Black women and men of all ages in four thousand schools before the system was dismantled in 1870.[12] The American Missionary Association (AMA) was active in Black education in succeeding decades, sending hundreds of people to start schools and teach Southern Blacks.[13]

The teaching by the AMA focused mainly on reading, writing, and arithmetic, because Southern educators were concerned about the practicality of education for Black men and women. Additionally, the 1896 *Plessy v. Ferguson* law crystallized the separate-but-equal stipulation but ignored the "equal" part; thus, conditions and resources in Black schools were generally subpar. Depending on their location and community support, some Black schools were more advanced than others. Overall, classes were extremely large and multi-age, supplies were short, and the teachers were often underprepared or underqualified.[14] In her oral history, Black educator and civil rights activist Septima Poinsett Clark said she did not learn much at Mary Street Elementary School in large part because of the class size: "There must have been a hundred children on that gallery; it was like a baseball stadium with the bleachers. You sat up on those bleachers. And the only thing I could see the teachers could do was to take you to the bathroom and back. By the time she got us all in the bathroom and back, it was about time to go home."[15]

Clark eventually left that school and went to one of the many home schools, which were often run by elderly Black women. She was held to high expectations for her learning, especially in spelling, *but public behavior remained a major focus of instruction*, both at school and at home. She recalled her mother's instructions about being a lady: "If you're going downtown for a common pin, it's nobody's business. And you dare not holler across the street. You're not supposed to [yell] across and say, 'Hey, Sally!' or 'Hey, Sue!' That's not the sign of a lady. And you never eat on the street."[16]

Clark's experience was typical for many Black women and girls in the late nineteenth and early twentieth centuries. Such school structures and family practices separated Black girls from their own authentic identities: it just wasn't acceptable to be anything other than what was considered "a lady," and the girls were not often afforded an opportunity to go beyond basic education.

TEACHER PAY: BLACK WOMEN'S INVISIBILITY BY OPTICAL CLOAKING

Many of the teachers hired in the Freedmen's Bureau institutions were white and from the North. White men were typically employed as supervisors or teachers in the upper grades, and women (Black and white) almost always taught the lower grades. Only a few Black women were hired in bureau schools, and some evidence suggests that white women were preferred.[17] Many of these mission societies recognized Black teachers' effectiveness with Black children but chose to hire white teachers anyway.[18] Many Black women teachers were not hired because they had dependent children, yet white women teachers with children could be hired.[19] The Black teachers who were hired to work in mission schools were often assigned to segregated housing, lower grades, and remote schools.[20]

Black women teachers were the lowest-paid teachers in most Southern states, with Florida and South Carolina being particular offenders in this regard.[21] The usual justification for paying women less than men was that men had to deal with more discipline problems and women had less experience; sometimes education also contributed to the sex differential.[22] Thus, Black women's pay for teaching was low and their opportunity for professional advancement was insignificant; I describe this invisibility as "optical cloaking." Optical cloaking is a scientific technique that allows objects, as large as people, to be hidden in plain sight and makes invisibility a promising new reality. Black women teachers' contributions and worthiness of equal pay were hidden from view and eclipsed by intersectional systems, structures, ideologies, and norms of the day.

Whites often were not supportive of Black education, so Black students, teachers, and parents were frequently abused or threatened.[23] Black schools were sometimes burned down or excessively taxed, and some evidence suggests that Black male teachers were whipped and murdered and Black women were physically violated, whereas the worst repercussions a white female teacher in a Black school might experience was being ignored by the white community or being refused housing.[24] Despite these disadvantages, Black women as well as white women were increasingly drawn to teaching. Teaching was considered the most prestigious and highest-paying job to which Black women could aspire. So, by 1910, more than 17,000 Black women were teaching in the Southern states, outnumbering Black men in the field by more than three to one and making up 1 percent of the region's Black women working outside the home.[25]

MESSAGES FROM TEXTBOOKS: BLACK GIRLS' AND WOMEN'S INVISIBILITY BY OMISSION

The late nineteenth-century elementary education consisted of reading, writing, and arithmetic as well as morality and proper behavior, as was evident in the textbooks Black women and girls used.[26] Historian Ruth Miller Elson contends that nineteenth-century textbook writers were frequently far more concerned with children's moral development than with the cultivation of their minds.[27] Like their white peers, Black girls were expected to control their public behavior and defer to boys. In these textbooks, Black men and women were generally presented as happy and naive people who needed direction from whites to succeed; Black women were often described as weak and defenseless individuals in need of masculine guidance.[28] Following is an excerpt from a textbook that discusses the restrictions on female behavior that started in childhood:

> Because public speaking is highly improper for her, the girl is not to be trained in oratory, the most popular subject in her brother's curriculum. She is cautioned: Be good, sweet maid, and let who will be clever. Small girls should not engage in their brothers' activities. Even a little girl who wants to help her brother build a cart is restrained because it is not a proper employment for a young lady.[29]

The implicit and explicit messages in these textbooks were biased and made Black girls *invisible by omission.*

BLACK GIRL'S AND WOMEN'S INVISIBILITY THROUGH SOCIAL NORMS, SINGLE-AXIS UNDERSTANDING, AND DISILLUSIONMENT

The turn of the century brought a slight change in attitude toward Black people's education. Some middle-class whites thought industrial training would support the South's economy if Southern leaders ever decided to integrate.[30] Industrial education came into existence during Reconstruction, and its purpose was to make education practical and relevant to the lives of Black people.[31] The prototypes for industrial education for Blacks were the famous Hampton Institute in Virginia and Tuskegee in Alabama (founded by Booker T. Washington). Many felt that industrial education was designed to prevent Blacks from attaining economic and educational parity with whites.[32] W. E. B. Dubois, who promoted classical education, debated the issue of the best way to educate Black people with Booker T. Washington, who favored industrial education. In my study on the history of mathematics education of Blacks during segregation, I point out that for far too long, these two great Black educators were pitted against each other in the Black history of education literature, and that the debate resulted in more rhetoric and commentary that "ultimately portrayed a political context, rather than what was actually happening in the classroom."[33] The fact was that not every Black person was ready to take on a classical education, given the high illiteracy rates after the Civil

War. Thus, education had to take both paths to establish a literate Black community focused on economic and political concerns.[34]

Most Black industrial institutions were coeducational, although the curriculum and extracurricular activities were gendered.[35] At industrial institutions such as Hampton and Tuskegee, Black young women received home economics education and focused on trades like tailoring or millinery (hat making) since the education beyond academics centered on their perceived future roles as wives and mothers.[36] For the most part, sex differentiation among Black women and girls was similar to what their white counterparts faced, except that Black women did not experience the opposition to their working outside the home that white women did.[37] Economic necessity forced many Black women to find employment, and "few people saw any illogic in assuming for many decades that it was acceptable for Black women, but not White ones to work outside the home."[38] Overall, although Southern educators and Northern industrialists were pleased to offer Black people an education that would improve their home life and living conditions, they ultimately had no intention of encouraging any alterations to the underlying economic and social structure of the South.[39]

By the 1950s, the debate about vocational education for Blacks had ended, but Black women's experiences in vocational education were still not equal to Black men's because sex was (and is) a factor in vocational choice. Many schools made concerted efforts to desegregate vocational programs by race, but substantial sex segregation remained just as salient as it had been in the nineteenth century.

This remained unchanged until 1972, when the Title IX law addressed sexism in education. Title IX states: "No person in the United States shall, on the basis of sex, be excluded from participation in, be denied the benefits of, or be subjected to discrimination under any education program or activity receiving Federal financial assistance."

This included vocational education. Nevertheless, as late as 1979, women were still enrolled mainly in traditional women's fields, such as home economics, cosmetology, and clerical work. Black girls and women remained invisible by being disillusioned because while race segregation was somewhat mediated, gender discrimination persisted.

MATHEMATICS RENDER BLACK GIRLS AND WOMEN INVISIBLE

Black girls' and women's education was (and still is) shaped by racialized and gendered norms and biases. In the preceding discussion, I described several ways Black women and girls have been made invisible in educational spaces: through their race and the associated stereotypes about their abilities, gender-based roles of wife and mother, the constrictions of "ladylike" behavior, being funneled into the lowest-level and lowest-paid teaching work, and being actively discouraged from pursuing any profession but teaching or a few typically female occupations. These examples shed light on how to consider their similar invisibility in mathematics. In this section, I present a *typology of invisibility for Black women and girls in mathematics* using the types discussed in the previous section. Figure 1.1 shows the different types of invisibility.

FIGURE 1.1 Invisibility typology of Black girls and women in mathematics and mathematics education

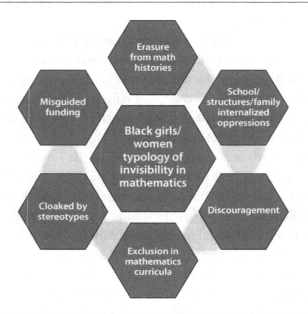

Mathematics Histories and Contemporary Stories Erase Black Women

Black girls and women are literately and figuratively erased from mathematics as a discipline and its history. In the literal sense, they are simply not there in critical masses throughout the P–20 educational pipeline.[40] The doctoral level is especially important because at this stage the academy and industry hire for positions, which come with a certain degree of power and decision-making. Why do so few Black women become mathematics faculty? One reason is that students in US schools never learn about Black women in mathematics, and rarely do they have Black women mathematics teachers.[41] Other reasons include either not surviving or being pushed out of the K–12, postsecondary, or graduate pipelines. Specifically, they deal with racialized and gendered micro- and macroaggressions, instructors not believing in their abilities, and the mental and physical tax of constantly having to prove themselves to others.[42]

Some Black women have achieved in mathematics, but their stories are largely unknown. The 2016 film *Hidden Figures* is a Hollywood recounting of the stories of Katherine Johnson, Mary Jackson, and Dorothy Vaughan, three Black women mathematicians who worked at the National Aeronautics and Space Administration (NASA) during the space race. The story is inspirational and life affirming, yet the film suggests that the high point of their lives was earning the respect of whites. White ontological expansiveness erased their talent and intellect.[43] Shannon Sullivan describes *white ontological expansiveness* as a habit of white privilege that considers geographical, linguistic, educational, economic, spiritual, and other spaces rightfully available for white inhabitation. Roni Ellington points out that this type of expansiveness promotes an unspoken and taken-for-granted license for whites to inhabit and dominate the spaces they occupy, even when these spaces are populated by people of color.[44]

Thirty other Black women with degrees in mathematics also worked at NASA at that time. This was a time of segregation, so we know that these Black women and many others in the South received their education largely at Historically Black Colleges and Universities (HBCUs). What was portrayed as exceptional was actually the norm, but many whites, particularly in the 1950s and 1960s, would not acknowledge such a claim, in part because it would mean that Black people are just as intelligent and capable as whites, if not more so.

Mathematics Tracking and Family Internalized Oppression

Black women's and girls' invisibility in mathematics is identifiable in US school structures (i.e., tracking) and protective family attitudes. Tracking, the process of sorting students by perceived ability, has been a part of the US school system since the 1930s, particularly in mathematics, although I would argue that it dates all the way back to ideas of Plato in his hierarchical society of philosophers, guardians, and merchants.[45] Tracking is a deep-seated structure with great consequences and rewards, depending on which track a student takes. Black students are often relegated to schools that either do not offer Advanced Placement (AP) programs or that rarely enroll Black students in advanced math courses.[46] A poignant example is the *Daniel v. California* court case. In July 1999, a young Black girl named Rasheda Daniel and three of her peers at Inglewood High School brought a class-action suit against the state of California challenging inequitable access to AP courses.[47] They cited differential access to AP classes that denied a class of primarily low-income students of color equal opportunity. Rasheda's school had three AP courses, but none were in mathematics or science, whereas other nearby public high schools, such as Beverly Hills and Arcadia, which served large numbers of white and affluent students, offered more than fourteen AP courses, among them calculus and physics.[48] This case demonstrated that there is in fact unequal access to mathematics and science courses and achievement for Black students, and this unequal access remains a serious, self-evident problem in our education system. Rasheda lost her case.

Historically, many Black families internalized the false idea that the professions were "aristocratic spheres to which Negroes should not aspire."[49] In addition to professions such as medicine and the law, Blacks were also discouraged and dissuaded from taking up "designing, drafting, architecture, engineering and chemistry," now known as science, technology, engineering, and mathematics (STEM) fields.[50] Because many Black families told their children that whites would not hire them in these professions and therefore their education would go to waste, few students focused on these areas. Of these, most were Black men, not women. Internalized oppression among Black families contributed to Blacks' invisibility in the STEM professions, especially Black women.

But even in a more contemporary context, Black families have complex relationships with mathematics. For example, in his dissertation, Danny B. Martin conducted analysis with Black parents and community members to better understand their beliefs about and meanings for mathematics. What he found was that for some of the participants he interviewed, their beliefs about mathematics developed in parallel to the development of their Black identities.[51] One specific participant, Harold, recognized the importance of mathematics as a school subject and for its importance for everyday life, but his early life experiences with racism, discrimination, and other barriers significantly affected his mathematics identity in negative ways such "that he no longer believed that he, and to some degree his 17-year-old son, could become meaningful participants in mathematics."[52]

Discouragement in Mathematics

Hidden in plain sight suggests that the object or person is deliberately overlooked. At the graduate level of mathematics, research suggests that Black women are not encouraged to participate in communities of practice that increase their persistence and success.[53] Some white faculty completely ignore and discourage Black women in their graduate programs.[54] In their study of the undergraduate and graduate experiences of twelve Black women mathematicians, Viveka Borum and Erica Walker found that regardless of their undergraduate institution (HBCU or non-HBCU), the women's graduate experiences were fraught with discrimination and lack of support.[55] A few women in the study reported feeling that the mathematics faculty did not care whether they obtained their doctorate degree or not; this was especially true in the larger graduate programs. For the women who had previously attended an HBCU, their transition to a mainstream, white-dominated environment was more difficult because class sizes were larger, and the nurturing component found at most HBCUs was greatly diminished. Several women in the study decided to leave their graduate institutions with a master's and pursued a doctorate somewhere else. A key word they used to describe their experiences was *traumatic*. They said that the treatment they received "damaged their self-esteem and made them unsure if they could ever receive a doctorate in mathematics."[56] Black women in graduate mathematics programs can remain invisible in plain sight due to the racism and sexism pervading these programs.

Exclusion in Mathematics Curricula

In a Twitter feed about *Hidden Figures*, several people asked why they had never learned about "those incredible Black women" in their history books. Textbooks generally exclude Black women's contributions to mathematics. I imagine that there have been many Black women who have made contributions to mathematics or mathematics education, but most Americans will never know about them because of the white supremacy and patriarchy that prevails in this country: white males have decided and often still do decide what is worth knowing, especially in mathematics and science. Who makes mathematics textbook decisions? I will discuss this later in the book.

Textbooks are one type of resource for teaching mathematics. Many other learning materials are available online, including sources that mathematics teachers can use to combat myths about who can do mathematics and to document women's contributions to mathematics. For example, *Mathematically Gifted and Black* is an online network of minorities whose mission is to feature and share the accomplishments of Blacks in the mathematical sciences.[57] Situating the learning of mathematics content within a context that describes accomplished mathematicians from all ethnic and racial groups can help students see connections beyond school. Students can also better understand that teachers are teaching people mathematics, rather than teaching mathematics to people. When Black women and girls do not see themselves in the curriculum, the message they receive is that they do not belong in mathematics.

Cloaked by Stereotypes

Black women and girls are hampered by intersectional stereotypes in mathematics. One stereotype positions Black women and girls as loud, aggressive, and not smart.[58] Stereotypes are dangerous because they assume one narrative, one story, and as Nigerian writer Chimamanda Ngozi Adichie points out, there is danger in a single story.[59] Adichie says that we cannot talk about the single story without talking about power. She points out that how stories are told, who tells them, and when they are told all depend on power. According to Adichie, "power is the ability not just to tell the story of another person [or group of people], but to make it the definitive story of that person or group." Consequently, these stories, or stereotypes, about Black women and girls persist and are difficult to dismantle.

Some mathematics teachers fail to see Black girls as science and mathematics achievers because they are so focused on Black girls' behaviors, thereby positioning them negatively. For example, in their three-year longitudinal study of how African American girls position themselves in relation to science and mathematics learning from fifth to seventh grade, including the impact of the positioning of teachers, counselors, and parents on this process, Rose Pringle et al. found that certain math teachers perceive Black girls as having limited mathematical knowledge and as bringing social challenges to the learning environment.[60] In a different study, Stephanie Jones found that third-grader Patti was infrequently afforded the opportunity to develop as a mathematics doer, while simultaneously being fully human in her Black girlhood, recognizing that mathematics classrooms uphold and promote white, middle-class values and identities.[61] Patti's teacher described Patti as "big," "aggressive," and "loud" and not characterizing her as a strong mathematics student, despite Jones recognizing Patti as such.[62] The way the teachers positioned Patti in the classroom also manifested itself in the afterschool math club created by Jones as a hybrid space where intersectional identities were promoted and valued, yet the other girls positioned Patti as a troublemaker and avoided her because they too cloaked Patti with stereotypes. These so-called social challenges are directly connected to Black girl stereotypes.

Misguided Funding

Of the billions of dollars being spent by federal and private organizations such as the National Science Foundation (NSF) to broaden participation in STEM fields beyond whites and Asians, only a small fraction is devoted to including Black girls and women.[63] More importantly, the national discussion about Black girls and women and STEM is not changing, and they remain underrepresented and pushed out of STEM fields. A 2017 search of active NSF awards using the keywords *Black women STEM* showed 11,488 hits. A search using *African American women STEM* yielded 34,506 abstracts focused on Black women and girls and STEM. Yet, underrepresentation and retention issues continue to plague the field. One reason for this is that the large majority of the NSF programs and interventions focused on the wrong issues—consistently addressing what STEM researchers and scholars think is wrong with Black girls themselves—rarely disrupting systems, structures, ideologies, and norms that exist in the mathematics discipline (i.e., white supremacy and patriarchy).

CONCLUSION

This chapter explored six types of invisibility that are not mutually exclusive, but dynamic and interrelated. Developing and unpacking a systematic classification of Black girls' and women's invisibility in mathematics and education more generally is important for setting the context for the rest of the chapters in *Making Black Girls Count in Math Education*. Illuminating the different ways they are invisible meets critics and skeptics at the front door; it may not stop them from focusing on things such as Black girls underpreparedness or their family's socioeconomic status and mother's highest level of education, but it warrants a different conversation—a conversation that involves much courage and political will. Situating mathematics learning environments, curricula, pedagogies, assessment, teacher education, and policies within this sociopolitical-historical context of invisibility makes for a complex narrative, one that is intersectional and seeks to uncover the role power and privilege play in our US mathematics education system.

2

MATHEMATICS LEARNING
ENVIRONMENTS AND BLACK GIRLS

Shifting the "Climate" Paradigm
from Dehumanizing to Human Flourishing

A classroom learning environment includes more than physical space; it consists of the entire learning setting, including instructional processes, materials used for instruction, student attitudes, and teacher-student, teacher-teacher, and student-student relationships.[1] We also know from research that learning environments can be conceptualized as the teacher's or student's subjective perceptions of their learning setting.[2] Previous studies have shown that the perceived learning environment is significantly related to student achievement as well as emotional and social outcomes.[3] Using multilevel modeling of data from 1,623 students from 69 classes (grades 5–10), Anne Frenzel and colleagues found significant relationships between students' perception of their mathematics classroom environment and their experiences of enjoyment, anxiety, anger, and boredom in mathematics.[4] They conducted this study in the German state of Bavaria, and the data corpus included all three German school types (vocational, general, and academic) ensuring social class, not intersectional variation. However, while this study was conducted outside the US context, the measure itself was validated, and I would be curious to see how Black girls' scores on these measures nuance Frenzel and colleagues' findings. Their empirical study provides an opening into thinking about what mathematics learning environments can be when we push back on conventional understandings and choose to investigate the role of social and emotional learning in mathematics.

Social and emotional learning are important constructs for some Black girls, as previous research showed that when Black girls in high school described their empowering experiences with mathematics teachers, they noted the importance of bonding with their mathematics teachers in fun and relaxing ways, while also engaging in rigorous mathematics.[5] Therefore, this chapter's central question is "What types of mathematics classroom environments and climates support and sustain Black girls' joy?"

Creating and sustaining mathematics learning environments for Black girls' enjoyment is a radical social project, because mathematics classroom environments were not necessarily designed with Black girls in mind; in fact, typical US mathematics learning environments were constructed and continue to be constructed in ways that privilege white middle-class students, since these environments instantiate the human interactions, standpoints, values, and interests of whiteness.[6] I use Tema Okun's white supremacy culture (WSC) framework to deconstruct and discuss key characteristics of US mathematics learning environments that make it a white space and inhospitable for many students but especially for Black girls.[7] The second half of the chapter draws imaginativeness from teacher learning expert Ilana Horn's motived classrooms framework, life virtues from mathematician Francis Su's teaching mathematics for human flourishing, and Norman Alston's concept of mathematics renaissance.[8] The intersection of these scholars' work with Black girlhood fashion an innovative opportunity to advance mathematics learning climates and environments that can center Black girl joy. Black girl joy is the internal self-actualization of vibrancy, satisfaction, hope, self-worth, and self-love.

THE MATHEMATICS LEARNING ENVIRONMENT AS A SOCIAL CONSTRUCT

Mathematics learning environments in the United States reflect the ideologies and norms of WSC; thus they are social constructs. Our mathematics communities have created and perpetuated these norms and ideas. Who are these communities? I am talking about the people who are considered a part of the "establishment"—senior university faculty and veteran high school mathematics teachers who have had long careers as mathematicians and department chairs. This establishment also includes popular mathematics curriculum developers and publishers, such as those that make the EdReports list.[9] White middle-class parents and other educational influencers represent this establishment of norms and ideas contributing to the national conversations about what mathematics is, who can do mathematics, who belongs in mathematics, and what does it mean to learn and be successful in mathematics. Decision-making power rests in the hands of the establishment, reflecting its principles, beliefs, and standards without consideration of historically marginalized communities of color, surely not Black girls' perspectives. This decision-making power has major influence and impact on how the larger society and mathematics educators perceive specific components of the learning environment as important for mathematics.

Dismantling Racism Works is a web-based workshop of resources and tools for understanding oppression in the United States from, specifically, race, racism and WSC systems.[10] I use these resources to bring to the fore, for the everyday person, the level of power the establishment holds in shaping mathematics education in the United States and ways Black girls are marginalized by this power. One of the components on the *Dismantling Racism Works* website features and identifies the characteristics that make up WSC. These characteristics are damaging because they are used as norms and standards without being proactively named, promote white supremacy thinking, and are destructive to both people of color and white people. When WSC is internalized by people of color, they become colluders to the perpetuation of whiteness; thus, to be clear, one does not need to be white to enact and believe in white supremacy logics. For example, a previous study proposed and employed a framework that characterized mathematics education as a white, patriarchal space to analyze undergraduate Black women's narratives of experience in navigating P–16 mathematics education.[11] Luis Leyva found that Black women's experiences of within-group tensions was a function of internalized racial-gendered ideologies, and the Black women normalized structural inequities in mathematics education buttressed by white supremacy culture.[12] But he also problematized their internalization of these logics by describing the variation in these Black women's resilience through coping strategies for managing such within-group tensions. Overall, internalizations are not our inevitable destiny; we have agency and the ability to resist and live into another version of ourselves.

Next I discuss four WSC characteristics embodied in mathematics learning environments, climates, and cultures: defensiveness, individualism, objectivity, and power hoarding. Within each section, I give details about why the characteristic is particularly problematic for Black girls and women.

Mathematics Climates Embody Defensiveness

The establishment of mathematics communities spends much energy defending against charges of racialized and gendered experiences by people of color instead of examining how these intersectional oppressions might actually be happening. For example, in their study that sought to understand seven university mathematics professors' perspectives about racialized and gendered experiences reported by students of color, the professors were defensive. Specifically, Taylor McNeill and colleagues found that some of the instructors' discourse was rooted in ideologies that mathematics is asocial and mathematical success is meritocratic, rendering racial and gendered systemic forces of oppression meaningless in undergraduate calculus.[13]

The establishment is also defensive about indictments of weed-out courses. Secondary and postsecondary mathematics teachers use courses, such as algebra and calculus, as the litmus test for advanced mathematics—if students cannot pass or struggle with these courses, then they are deemed not ready, underprepared, and often encouraged to choose a lower-level course (secondary) and non-STEM major (undergraduate). Open discussions about different ideas or ways to support such students are generally not an option, because faculty hold much power and authority. Even the general society can be defensive about who is or is not a "math person." Everyday citizens in the United States say with conviction that they cannot do mathematics or are not good at mathematics, yet when that statement is challenged to consider other factors, such as "you just had the wrong teacher," or "maybe the way math was taught was not relevant for your life," people can get defensive. They get defensive in large part because they have internalized the norms and ideologies of mathematics as an unbiased discipline, what smartness looks like in mathematics (e.g., quick answers, ability to memorize, get topics quickly without help) and have come to know themselves as not one of those people.

Black girls often find themselves enrolled in public schools where robust mathematics teaching and resources are limited.[14] Many are relegated to either the regular or low-level mathematics courses and thus are unable to experience liberatory pedagogies whereby they come to know themselves as curators of mathematics and critically conscious scholars. I am not suggesting that participation in advanced mathematics coursework guarantees liberatory experiences; the instruction and environment can be more open-ended and less constraining because there is an assumption that students enrolled in such courses deserve and are capable of that type of experience. Thus, in a system that values a particular scope and sequence of mathematics training, many Black girls are left out. When Black girls do not see themselves in the profiles and experiences that the establishment has created and promoted, they can develop internalized feelings of inferiority and eventually turn away from mathematics all together. For Black girls, the decision to turn away from mathematics is misguided because it is often based in myths of meritocracy. Unfortunately, many mathematics teachers adopt meritocratic, rather than complex stances to explain racialized disparities in mathematics achievement.[15]

For example, in a study that explored the experiences of two sixth-grade Black girls (Rachel and Stella) with middle-school mathematics and the impact of the sociocultural context on their motivation and mathematical identity, Jae Hoon Lim found that their mathematics teacher, Mrs. Oliver, did not have Stella's name on the recommend list for the seventh-grade pre-algebra class, even though Stella was enrolled in Mrs. Oliver's advanced sixth-grade mathematics class and had test scores and grades comparable to other high-achieving white peers in the class.[16] Mrs. Oliver defended this meritocratic decision when she suggested that Stella was not "working hard in her class, a factor that she often cited as the most important individual characteristic for learning higher mathematics."[17] Lim's analysis revealed: "She [Stella] continued to experience a feeling of difference, self-inadequacy, and even inferiority to other high-achieving White girls. This fostered in her mind a high level of anxiety, negative self-prophecy, and self-doubt about her ability to achieve excellence in the mathematics domain."[18]

It does not make sense that Stella had feelings of inferiority, given that she was enrolled in the advanced mathematics class and had the grades to demonstrate competence. But this points back to how Black girls experience intersectional oppression in mathematics spaces, and these experiences are common. In a different study, Shanyce Campbell used base year surveys from the Education Longitudinal Study of 2002 that offered a nationally representative sample of approximately 15,362 sophomores in public and private high schools across the United States.[19] She extrapolated the responses of 853 tenth-grade Black girls to examine the extent to which the role of Black girls' behaviors influenced their teachers' decisions to place them in advanced courses; her findings were similar to Lim's study. Campbell found students who participated every day were more likely to be recommended for honors or advanced courses, yet confident Black girls were less likely than their less confident peers to be recommended for these classes.[20] Campbell posits that Black girls who ask questions and routinely participate may overwhelm teachers who could then misinterpret their zeal for that of a student who does not fully understand the material. Lim's and Campbell's findings are confounding, but they do provide insights into the intersectional erasure Black girls' experience in mathematics. The messages to Black girls can be mixed. On one hand, they are being asked to participate more, but on the other hand, they are penalized for too much or certain types of participation. Overall, the findings show how the defensiveness of mathematics teachers in power creates oppressive cultures and decisions for Black girls. The defense mechanisms of math teachers leave ideologies, systems, and structures unexamined and unchallenged, therefore blaming the victim. It seems as if Black girls cannot win either way in our mathematics education system.

Individualism Is Privileged in Mathematics Learning Environments

Individualism is another characteristic of WSC. *Disrupting Racism Works* describes individualism as a desire for individual recognition and credit. Individualism is also characterized as a belief that people are responsible for solving problems alone. When people adopt individualistic perspectives, they think that accountability is vertical rather than horizontal with peers, often having limited comfort working as part of a team. Never having the opportunity to work as part of a team can lead to isolation, consequently giving more value to competition rather than cooperation. These descriptions depict typical US mathematics learning environments and is evidenced in textbooks, student goals, instruction, conferences, and other spaces.[21] Individualism in mathematics is also an ideology and existential experience manifested in the mind and body and can be debilitating for people who seek more communal and collective experiences.[22] Overall, mathematics learning environments perpetuate a consciousness that focuses on individualism as a source of empowerment.[23]

African American people are communal and expressive. Research by the former president of the National Council of Teachers of Mathematics, Robert Berry III, suggests that the mathematics learning instruction Black students receive is in opposition to these cultural styles and learning preferences.[24] My own empirical work with high school Black girls suggests that they value social interaction and the sharing of power in their mathematics classrooms and having those experiences can contribute to the development of positive mathematics identities, participation, persistence, and achievement.[25] Undergraduate and graduate Black women mathematicians can experience marginalization and isolation on the road to getting their mathematics degrees because of the ethos of individualism in mathematics departments.[26] Again, invoking Leyva's Black women undergraduate STEM majors investigation, he used his framework to show how individualism disrupts solidarity between Black women undergraduate STEM majors.[27] His innovative three-pronged framework detailed the ideological (disciplinary/organizational logics), relational (everyday interactions/individual labor), and institutional (access/representation) dimensions of mathematics contexts that contributed to these Black women working against each other, rather than helping one another.

Overall, individualism creates conditions and climates in mathematics that hurt Black girls and women; thus, there is a great need to challenge these logics and normalized inequities in order to "cultivate mathematics spaces where Black women's ideological differences are reconciled, and mathematical talent is celebrated."[28]

Objectivity and Austerity Are What Get Noticed and Rewarded in Mathematics Environments

In our everyday lives, people talk about being "objective." For example, when siblings argue, disagree, or fight, society says that parents should be objective when listening and gauging the issue to help their children solve the problem. Listening to both children share their version of the story would be considered an objective process. The reality is that the process is not completely objective without any type of bias. We know this because of several potential factors; the parent listened with many things in mind: they birthed these children, know them well—how they think, perceive things—and what the children need to feel better. So, in the parent's conversation with the siblings, they may recall previous situations and consider the context, and create a way of communicating with the siblings so that each one perceives that an objective process has occurred. Objectivity is difficult to achieve because all knowledge and decisions are informed by personal values, interests, and ideas. Western scientific methods promote objectivity in their paradigms and suggest that researchers start the process of inquiry by excluding social factors from the production of knowledge.[29] But several philosophers have critiqued this position pointing out that *all knowledge* is socially constructed and reflects human interests, values, and action. The knowledge that people create is heavily influenced by their interpretations of their experiences and their positions within particular social, economic, and political systems and structures of society.[30]

While WSC believes in objectivity, the *Disrupting Racism Works* resources highlight that objective thinking believes that emotions are inherently destructive and irrational and should not play a role in decision-making or group processes. Objectivity invalidates people who show emotion and require people to think in a linear and austere ways, while ignoring or invalidating those who think in other ways. Finally, objectivity is impatient with any thinking that does not appear "logical" to those with power.[31] Philosopher Sandra Harding challenges this thinking by purposing what she calls "strong objectivity."[32] Harding suggests that social location and social factors are important for getting at strong objectivity because assumptions, values, interests are put on the table up front, rather than hidden.[33]

These characteristics of objectivity—rationality, no emotions, linearity—are a part of mathematics cultures, climates, and environments. Students perceived to be serious about their mathematics learning are efficient, precise, focused, serious, and logical. Innovation, solidarity, fun, and enjoyment are not welcome; still, these are the types of learning environments many Black girls desire. What is wrong with singing at the same time a Black girl is using algebra tiles to model with mathematics, one of the eight standards for mathematical practice.[34] Previous research and my lived experience as a mathematics teacher highlights the need for fun and a little excitement when learning mathematics.[35] In a blog that Dr. Ilana Horn and I wrote a few years ago, we pointed out that humor, especially in certain forms, is not welcome in schools and mathematics classrooms.[36] Some educators use this label with derision, assuming students step into this role for negative reasons, like avoiding work or garnering attention that distracts from lessons, making the teacher's job harder. But this is not always the case. One of the most beautiful illustrations of joy and humor is a video from the Counting Collections project at UCLA, led by Dr. Megan Franke.[37] The video is of a kindergarten or first-grade Black girl responding to her teacher, who asked the class how they might count a large set of items. The young Black girl responded with much fervor, glee, and with a big smile on her face, "I can count by 30s!" That is the type of excitement and joy that should be a part of learning mathematics. This type of disposition is not always considered "rigorous," so when some Black girls bring these pieces of their humanity to the learning of mathematics, their identities can become fragmented. Consequently, they can get shunned, overlooked, and characterized as students not interested, serious, or diligent in their mathematics learning.

Power Is Rarely Shared in Mathematics Learning Environments

Finally, power hoarding is a characteristic of WSC and prevalent in mathematics environments and climates. Power hoarding means those who have it see no value in sharing power; they also see power as a limited resource—that there is only so much to go around. People with power often feel threatened when anyone suggests changes in how things should be done, be it in a school, a community, or a mathematics classroom. The feeling of a threat stems from the power holder's perspective that changes are suggested because it reflects their leadership. *Disrupting Racism Works* points out that those with power do not see themselves as hoarding power, but rather that they have the best interests of the organization, students, department, and so on at heart and assume those wanting change are ill-informed (stupid), emotional, and inexperienced. Mathematics instructors are trained in their programs about content, not pedagogy, so oftentimes their dispositions are steeped in the notion that they are the only knowledge holders in addition to the textbooks. Paulo Freire called it "banking education," the notion that teachers' roles are to deposit information, in this case, mathematics concepts, into students' heads.[38] Nothing about this type of teaching is transformative; students should be co-constructors of mathematical knowledge. Power hoarding can be examined on different levels from the micro classroom (e.g., teachers seldom letting students talk) to the macro ideologies and structures in mathematics education (e.g., severe underrepresentation or under-retention in doctoral mathematics programs because faculty rarely view women or minorities as capable).

Looking through Black girl specificity, sharing power is important and can contribute to Black girls' positive mathematics identities because when power is shared, they see themselves in a different light: that they are capable of developing into strong mathematicians and being recognized as such by peers and their teachers.[39] Power hoarding by mathematics instructors begins early and continues all the way to postsecondary education. In Leyva and colleagues' study of Black students' perceptions of introductory mathematics instruction as a racialized and gendered experience at a large, public, and historically white research university, they found that Black students perceived calculus instruction entrenched in an exclusionary logic that faculty hold more mathematical power than students.[40] When this collides with racial and gender stereotypes and underrepresentation in STEM, Black students face inequitable opportunities to participate in the classroom because they are positioned as lacking intellectual authority. All in all, power hoarding is a part of WSC, pervasive in mathematics learning environments, and oppressive for Black girls and women.

CREATING BLACK GIRL JOY IN MATHEMATICS LEARNING ENVIRONMENTS AND CLIMATES

The inspiring work of Alston's conceptualization of an urban mathematics renaissance, Horn's motivational framework, and Su's conceptualization of mathematics for human flourishing suggests how white supremacy cultures and climates might be dismantled and how to create conditions for Black girl joy and liberation in mathematics.[41] What is beautiful about these three frames of reference is that at their intersection with Black girlhood, they provide the reader a view of what is possible for creating powerful mathematics learning environments for Black girls beyond the white gaze.

Social, Emotional, and Academic Intersection of Mathematics Learning Environments for Black Girls

In our study of humanizing teaching and learning for Black girls, Norman Alston described a concept he called the *urban mathematics renaissance*:

> It would be the intellectual crown jewel of the city. It would be filled with exhibits that children would be drawn to and inspired by. It would be staffed by people who love children, teaching, and learning . . . [O]ur country needs a revival, a rebirth of simply learning and doing mathematics for its own sake. Not for a test score, not for a grade, and not for admission into some college. We simply need to learn that mathematics can be enjoyed the same way you'd enjoy literature, the arts, entertainment, or athletics.[42]

as opportunities to grow and learn, and support for helping Black girls recognize their own mathematical strengths. *Accountability* is the fourth feature of a motivational mathematics classrooms and accounts for how we support Black girls to be invested in their own learning as well as the learning of their peers. Horn contends that accountability is not about assessment, but "structures and routines that oblige students to report, explain, or justify their activities."[49] Giving Black girls some say in their activities that they engage in for mathematics class and helping them to see the relationship between those activities and their personal goals gives them a greater perception of commitment to accomplishing those goals. Last, *autonomy*, or student-organized resources (e.g., time, peers, teachers, textbooks, manipulatives, etc.) for making sense of their work and following through is an important consideration for motivational mathematics classrooms. Black girls need opportunities to pursue their own curiosities and contribute to the classroom community, because when they do, they are more likely to experience deeper conceptual learning, seek out intellectual challenges, and nerd out on academic work.

Horn states that autonomy can be inculcated by "linking instruction to students' strengths and interests, giving meaningful reasons for learning different content, allowing students the time they need to learn, and valuing different ways of thinking about ideas."[50] Teachers implementing these features in their mathematics classrooms with Black girls can ensure what I call a "holistic motivation" because it would mean working in solidarity with Black girls, considering their social realities through broader sociopolitical contexts, and attuning to the social and emotional conditions that many Black girls need to participate effectively in mathematical activities.

Play, Beauty, Truth, Justice, and Love: Connecting Mathematics to Our Deepest Human Desires

Black girls participating effectively in mathematics activities for the purpose of flourishing in their lives is empowering. Learning and participating in mathematics for human flourishing outcomes was advanced by mathematician Francis Su and provides innovational fodder for imagining conditions for Black girl joy and liberation in mathematics. In his talk at the Mathematical Association of America–American Mathematical Society Joint Math Meetings conference, Su asked an important question to a room full of his fellow professional mathematicians: "How can the deeply human themes that drive us to do mathematics be channeled to build a more beautiful and just world in which all can truly flourish?" He constructed this question and idea and deemed it worthy of exploration with his colleagues after he had received a letter from Christopher, an African American high school dropout serving a thirty-two-year sentence in a high-security federal prison right outside of Atlanta. Su's words are thought provoking and striking, particularly when he said:

> Right now, you've probably formed a mental image of who Christopher is, and you might be wondering why I'm opening my speech with his story. When you think about who does mathematics—both who is capable of doing mathematics and who wants to do mathematics—would you think of Christopher? And yet he wrote me a letter after seven years in prison. He said: "I've always had a proclivity for mathematics, but being in a very early stage of youth and also living in some adverse circumstances, I never came to understand the true meaning and benefit of pursuing an education . . . over the last three years I have purchased and studied a multitude of books to give me a profound and concrete understanding of Algebra I, Algebra II, College Algebra, Geometry, Trigonometry, Calculus I and Calculus II." Christopher was writing me for help in furthering his mathematics education. When you think of who does mathematics, would you think of Christopher? Every being cries out silently to be read differently.[51]

The last words of Su's statement, "Every being cries out silently to be read differently," are significant for thinking about Black girls and mathematics learning. Black girls do cry out to be read differently because of the ways societal stereotypes have overshadowed and eclipsed their genius. Su is unapologetically challenging the establishment about who does mathematics. Next, I use his five human flourishing concepts to build out mathematics learning environments that can support Black girls' mathematics development.

"PLAY" DEVELOPS BLACK GIRLS' HOPEFULNESS, COMMUNITY, AND PERSEVERANCE

Play belongs in mathematics learning environments because it can help Black girls flourish. Su argues that one cannot flourish without play. Black girls enjoy play. One of my studies argued for further research of this notion of creating a space for play for Black girls to be happy, gregarious, social, and "goofy" (an adjective one of the participants used).[52] One high school Black girl participant detailed that she likes to play "in-between time." "We know how to have fun and get the work, the job done. We do it in-between, like we'll be doing work with a joke here and there but still we understand and get the work done."[53] This quote suggests that Black girls understand that there is a time and place for play. But Su is pushing this idea further. He suggests that mathematics instructors should "play up" the role of play in how they teach and who they teach. An environment of play can be harder than one of lecture style because teachers and instructors must be able to think on their feet, ready for anything to happen. Su points out that it is play that makes inquiry-based learning so effective.

Because play builds life virtues such as hopefulness, community, and perseverance, it is necessary for Black girls. The level of harm Black girls are expected to overcome in order to receive an education in the United States is astounding; when that harm follows them into mathematics classrooms, it stunts their development into mathematicians. So, mathematics teachers and instructors should include different ways to embed play into the ethos of the environment for Black girls, such as relaxed environments with the invitation of play while working. Fun puzzles and games as a type of play-oriented activity can keep them interested in mathematics. When they are interested, they build hope that they can solve hard problems. When Black girls are excited about their interests in mathematics and what they are learning, they share it with their friends, families, and peers, and that sharing builds community. Sticking with mathematics investigations on a consistent basis builds up Black girls' problem-solving muscles to persevere, even when success is delayed. So, overall, mathematics environments filled with play supports Black girls' mathematics development and participation.

DIVERSE CONCEPTUALIZATIONS OF "BEAUTY" IN MATHEMATICS CAN BUILD BLACK GIRL JOY

If mathematics is for human flourishing, we must help Black girls see its beauty. Su quickly points out that hegemonic characterizations of beauty in mathematics are limited but should be expanded to include other ways to motivate through beauty; for example, the use of art, music, and patterns can be used to illuminate the elegance of simple but significant ideas, and the wondrous applicability of these ideas to the real world in different fields.[54] One profound example of motivating mathematics learning through these expanded understandings of beauty is the Supporting Computational Algorithmic Thinking or SCAT project. In Jakita Thomas's National Science Foundation CAREER Award, she worked with twenty-three middle-school Black girls in the Atlanta area, over seven years, to expose them to game design, a technological field in which Black girls and women are severely underrepresented.[55] Thus, to address this technology gap, she advanced an important on-ramp concept for developing critical thinking skills called computational algorithmic thinking (CAT)—the ability to identify and understand a problem, articulate an algorithm or set of algorithms in the form of a solution to the problem, implement that solution in such a way that the solution solves the problem, and evaluate the solution based on some set of criteria.

In Thomas's program, middle-school Black girls developed CAT capabilities as they worked in dyads engaging in the game design cycle (i.e., brainstorming, storyboarding, physical prototyping, design documenting, and implementation) to collaboratively design increasingly complex games that addressed a range of social justice issues they chose, ranging from gun violence to environmental sustainability. Creating video games that reflected the viewpoint of the communities in which the girls lived and the world around them was one way of cultivating joy and transcendence (the ability to embrace mystery), two virtues Su suggests develop from pursuing mathematics through beauty. Although some of the girls struggled initially with learning CAT, over the course of the longitudinal study, they persevered and improved.[56] Ultimately, the girls created sophisticated and beautiful protypes of their games, and the program supported the girls to master more advanced computational thinking, an essential skill for most STEM careers. All save one of the original twenty-three girls in the SCAT program went on to attend college majoring in STEM fields.[57]

BLACK GIRL JOY AND THE QUEST FOR TRUTH IN MATHEMATICS THROUGH RIGOROUS THINKING, HUMILITY, AND CIRCUMSPECTION

Mathematics learning environments that promote the quest for truth as an exercise in rigorous thinking and humility can support Black girls' mathematics development. Su points out that engaging in mathematics is a quest for truth because we do not do science to confirm declarative statements, but rather our investigations are questions for which the answer is not so clear. Many middle and high school mathematics teachers do not encourage an ethos of exploration and uncertainty, but rather a set of rules, facts, and procedures that have already been accepted as truth in society. Previous research has shown that it takes mathematics teachers who not only understand content but also have pedagogical knowledge. Additional competencies are needed when it comes to Black girls, such as understanding their social realities and the history of racial and gendered experiences in mathematics.[58] Black girls want to be challenged in mathematics and positioned as knowers of mathematical ideas.[59] Presenting interesting problems to Black girls or, better yet, having them identify problems in the world that they care about and want to explore, is one way to get at the mining of rigorous thinking. Su defines rigorous thinking as the ability to handle ideas well and craft clear arguments with those ideas; he suggests that the ability to reason in the public space, such as activist work, should be promoted. Using mathematics to model patterns Black girls see in their schools or local communities is one way to begin this work.

Working with social studies teachers to create essential questions about the patterns the girls find interesting and worthy of study is another example of how mathematics can be used in this quest for truth process. Mathematics and social studies teachers collaborating in solidarity with Black girls on problems they want to investigate is an effective strategy. However, mathematics and social studies teachers must exercise caution and collaborate in this work only after they have engaged in deep critical interrogation of US systems and structures buttressed by whiteness and racialized and gendered oppression. Not doing this first step can result in the design of dangerous curriculum, such as the one created with the use of slave content by teachers in California, Georgia, and New York. This topic is examined in depth in chapter 3 about mathematics curriculum.

Finally, Su contends that mathematics teachers must model the virtue of humility in their teaching and be explicit with their students about how they plan to utilize mathematics to cultivate humility, a disposition that serves everyone in their entire lives. One of the best ways to model this notion of humility is to embrace when our arguments are wrong or incomplete. When teachers make this practice a normative part of the learning environment, students are more likely to take risks and try harder. Arguments have limits, and thus through the virtue of circumspection, we train ourselves to not overgeneralize. This is another opportunity for which mathematics teachers might engage Black girls. Stereotypes are a generalization, and it would be a productive exercise to discuss with Black girls how stereotypes about Black girls as a "category" or Black people in general originate and are sustained. Helping them to understand that counternarratives are important data points is a compelling method-ological technique for pushing back on stereotypes. Overall, teaching mathematics as a quest for truth in order to develop rigorous thinking, humility, and circumspection could prove transformative for Black girls when those quests stem from ideas they generate.

JUSTICE-ORIENTED CLIMATES CAN DEVELOP BLACK GIRL FLOURISHING

Justice is required for human flourishing; we flourish when we treat others justly and are treated in just ways. Su conceptualizes justice as setting things right and points out how powerful of a motivator justice can be in action. Mathematicians and mathematics teachers have much work to do in correcting injustices, which starts with changing how they view racialized, gendered, and other marginalized students. I suggest that there are levels of justice, including the micro, meso, and macro. Micro-level justice could include the disruption of the one-on-one, daily practices mathematics instructors engage in (thinking those practices are neutral), such as telling students that they should drop their class if they cannot comprehend the material fast enough.[60] An example of a meso-level practice that mathematics instructors need to make right is the use of mathematics curricula that perpetuate Eurocentric perspectives and contributions. Su highlights the fact that even when people are equitable (i.e., mathematics instructors), even if they desire to be impartial, US society (macro) is not just if its structures and practices are not also just. Our mathematics education system, P–20, is wrought with structures that are unjust because they hurt and oppress racialized and marginalized students, Black girls and women specifically.

So, creating mathematics climates through a justice-centric ethos can develop Black girl joy. At the micro level, building authentic and trusting relationships with Black girls can foster their interest in mathematics because space has been made to bring their humanity into the classroom and learning enterprise. Building trusting and authentic relationships with Black girls is an act of justice—setting things straight—because we know that Black girl stereotypes continue to get in the way of mathematics teachers viewing them as capable for learning rigorous mathematics.[61] Establishing a climate of justice as reflected through project-based learning is an example of a meso-level strategy. Mathematics instructors should look around them to notice that Black girls and women are missing, indicating that instructors and faculty are not teaching mathematics to help Black girls and women flourish. Action such as bringing together faculty to discuss and setting goals for not only ways to recruit more Black girls into mathematics, but also ways to retain and sustain them is a just act. One way of doing that is to tear down exclusionary practices: weed-out courses, denying Black girls admission, insurmountable comprehensive exams, and privileging white male students for coauthorship on manuscripts, grants, and conferences. Su summarizes the role of justice for supporting Black girls' flourishing:

> Let me be clear: there is no good reason to tell a student she doesn't belong in math. That's the student's decision. Not yours. You see the snapshot of her progress, but you don't see her trajectory. You can't know how she will grow and flourish in the future. But you can help her get

there. Of course, you should give forthright counsel to students about skills they might need to develop further if they want to go on in mathematics, but if you see mathematics as a means to help them flourish, why wouldn't you encourage them to take more math?[62]

The indictment in this quote is one to take seriously. Black girls and women deserve the same level of investment mathematics faculty and instructors provide to white and Asian (Chinese/Japanese) students. Su goes on to say that having an advocate, a faculty member who says, "I see you, and I think you have a future in math," is significant for underrepresented groups who already have so many voices telling them they cannot. If we teach mathematics to help Black girls flourish, then we should not set up structures that negate them for sometimes having weaker backgrounds, for example, or make them feel out of place because faculty are the shepherds of mathematics culture.

BLACK GIRL JOY IN MATHEMATICS THROUGH LOVE

Su's final desire of human flourishing is love. Love is the greatest human desire. Su contends that to love and be loved is a supreme mark of human flourishing and that it serves the other desires—play, truth, beauty, and justice—and it is served by them. Black girls and women cry out silently to be read differently, yet we continue as a mathematics community and society generally to freeze them in time—through our biases, assumptions, and hegemonic perspectives about who can do mathematics and who belongs in mathematics. Love means being able to say, "What are you going through?" It means inviting pain and suffering into the learning space, because Black girlhood theories suggest that to understand Black girls in all their full humanity, we must not separate the social and emotional from the academic—they are intersectional and multidimensional. And yes, such questions belong in a mathematics classroom if it is for human flourishing. Overall, Black girls need their mathematical experiences to involve these aspects of love.

3

THE CARTOGRAPHY OF MATHEMATICS CURRICULA THROUGH BLACK GIRLHOOD GEOGRAPHIES

I n the summer of 2020, a senior program officer from the K–12 solutions unit at the Bill and Melinda Gates Foundation invited me to participate in several design charrettes for a mathematics curricula efficacy and enactment study. The program officer explained that Gates was investing in research to better understand the contribution of mathematics curricula to student outcomes, as well as what conditions contribute to the beneficial use of those instructional materials by teachers (e.g., kinds and levels of professional development, school- and district-level conditions). The Gates Foundation recognized that education research has not always translated into valuable insights for the field, so it was trying something different with this new project. It launched a *collaborative process to design the research* (charrettes) to ensure the project resulted in meaningful insights for students, their teachers, and schools. It provided an initial theory of change to approach the research, which included context, curricula transformations, and outcomes. Specifically, its theory of change suggested that each mathematics curriculum is implemented in a context—a set of schools within a district that has plans and priorities for students' mathematics achievement, accountability measures for students and teachers, and operates within a limited set of resources.

The theory of change also included the *transformation of curricula* from what is intended for delivery in the publisher's materials to what is, first, planned by teachers for delivery and then ultimately delivered or enacted to students in the classroom.[1]

The final component of the project's theory of change captured the outcomes—how teachers transform the curriculum, teachers' skills in delivering high-quality mathematics instruction, and their attitudes and views about students' capabilities. In the end, how teachers enact instruction is what will affect the students—the quality of their work; the equity of opportunity provided to students for engaging in deep, conceptual understanding of mathematics content, and their mathematics achievement. Some of the initial research questions included:

- Which math curricula (i.e., Eureka, Illustrated Math, Ready Math, and McGraw Hill California Math) have greater impact on student outcomes, for which students and in what contexts? What are the characteristics of the more effective curricula?
- What distinguishes the more successful curricula, including extent of fidelity of implementation, teacher characteristics, and professional supports?
- Across all the curricula, how and why does the alignment between the planned and enacted curriculum vary by specific curricula, school, types and coherence of supports, teacher characteristics and/or by student characteristics?

I opened the chapter with this academic professional experience because it provides a comprehensive understanding of what mainstream researchers in curriculum evaluation care about and therefore investigate—efficacy and enactment. The National Research Council commissioned a committee of mathematicians, mathematics educators, and methodologists to author a book discussing the reviews of the evaluation research literature that has accumulated around K–12 mathematics curricula. This committee collected, reviewed, and classified almost seven hundred studies, solicited expert testimony during two workshops, developed an evaluation framework, established dimensions or criteria for three methodologies (content analyses, comparative studies, and case studies), drew conclusions on the corpus of studies, and made recommendations for future research.[2] Needless to say, curricular efficacy and enactment are important processes to study because of their links to educational practice—the link between standards and accountability measures. We have been and continue to be in an era of accountability in which many schools, teachers, and students face sometimes severe consequences when they do not meet their state's annual progress benchmarks.

Schools meeting their yearly progress benchmarks is important, so understanding the role mathematics curricula play in that process is crucial. Overall, what we know from previous research is that a curriculum can support students' learning of rigorous mathematics, teachers rely heavily on curriculum materials as novices, and curriculum materials can be educative.[3] However, critical mathematics education scholars know that mainstream curricular materials can be constraining in that they are written for a general audience, which further privileges dominant views leaving many Black girls invisible.[4] This chapter explores the question, "How is Black girlhood suppressed by the epistemological processes and space of mathematics curricula?"

Epistemology is the study of knowledge, so what I mean by epistemological processes are the activities or methods for designing and choosing mathematics curricula. The epistemological space is the content, lessons, tasks, instructional routines, and assessments found in most mathematics curricula textbooks and teacher manuals. I explore this question by first using cartography or mapping to highlight factors influencing the design of mathematics curricula to students' opportunities to learn and what it can mean for Black girls' mathematics learning and development. I then discuss how because of the importance of mathematics curricular design and its connection to student learning, the work of schools and districts adopting their mathematics curriculum is complex and illustrative of hidden power relations. This complex process is rarely informed by empirical research problematizing Black girls' mathematics learning because the decision-makers seldom consider criticality.

In the end, the power a curriculum adoption committee holds is consequential because whichever mathematics curriculum materials are chosen for adoption becomes the official knowledge that teachers in thousands of state districts or schools across the country must enact with their students. The official mathematical knowledge is not culture-free and unbiased, but situated in long histories of educational inequalities, which makes it political. I discuss these politics associated with the official mathematics knowledge and the ways teachers take up and enact mathematics curricula. The chapter ends with a mathematics curricular vision for Black girlhood's journey into mainstream mathematics curricula design and outcomes, specifically what centering mathematics curricula of solidarity can do to push us forward in developing more liberatory mathematics education for Black girls. I am a Black girl cartographer.

DESIGNING MATHEMATICS CURRICULA FOR OPPORTUNITIES TO LEARN

Have you ever thought about who designs mathematics curricula and what the designers consider in creating those curricula? They consider learning theories, different philosophies of education, and historical and contemporary developments. For example, in the 1950s, after the Soviet Union put a satellite in space (*Sputnik*) first, the United States immediately created NASA and implemented a radical change in the way we taught mathematics and science. The curriculum changed to include more advanced mathematics topics to be taught at the elementary and secondary levels, such as number theory (i.e., counting in Base 2, in addition to Base 10). The curriculum shift was called "New Math." The main problem with New Math is it was designed with mathematics in mind, but not mathematical learning.[5]

As such, design is important because it can influence students' opportunities to learn and their outcomes. In a study that explored how the design features of curriculum materials might influence potential opportunities to learn and student outcomes, Janine Remillard, Barbara Harris, and Roberto Agodini conducted a comparative, documentary analysis of four popular mathematics curricula used in the United States (*Investigations*; *Scotts Foresman–Addison Wesley (SFAW)*; *Saxon Math*; *Math Expressions*).[6] I cite this foundational study because these four mathematics curricula are likely to be those used by Black girls in the

United States, since they are commonly found in many public schools. This study also provides a clear and foundational picture of *how* curricula effect students' opportunities to learn mathematics. As they compared the curricula, they specifically looked at: (a) mathematical emphasis, (b) instructional approach, and (c) support for teachers, each of which play a role in whether students get a chance to learn mathematics. Their results revealed substantially different types of opportunities to learn across the four sets of mathematics curriculum materials.

Mathematical emphasis means the knowledge that is valued in the curriculum. Remillard and colleagues examined the mathematical emphasis of the curricula by considering three components of the specific curriculum's daily lessons: (a) the conceptual level of mathematical tasks; (b) the use of regular routines that provide opportunities for engagement with concepts, facts, and procedures; and (c) the frequency of repeated practice to develop procedural fluency. They looked at twenty tasks for each of the four curricula and found that all four placed some level of emphasis on low-demand tasks, which consisted of memorization and procedures without connections, but *Saxon* and *Expressions* placed the most emphasis on this area. High-demand tasks included procedures with connections and doing mathematics (mathematics thinking and strategic competence); overall, *Investigations* placed the most focus on high-demand tasks, specifically doing mathematics.[7] These differences in emphasis are not just cognitively consequential for Black girls, but also have implications for their mathematical engagement. Many Black girls report that they want to be challenged in their mathematics classes, not just lectured at or doing worksheets.[8] In a study that explored middle-school Black girls' relationships with their middle-school mathematics teachers, Keonya Booker and Jae Hoon Lim found that the girls had stronger positive relationships with the mathematics teachers who used the curriculum to focus on making connections—what the authors called authentic pedagogy.[9] Authentic pedagogy uses instructional methodologies that make a mathematics curriculum relevant to students, provides real-life examples of how mathematics is important to future career success, and gives students opportunities to apply knowledge learned in transferable domains.[10] Dalia, one of the Black girls in their study, made the following comment about how she does mathematics in different domains, such as home cooking:

> I think the best way to learn math is . . . like I say with decimals, to help me think of other things . . . like money that has a decimal in it, or fractions like on measurement cups and stuff. I like to cook a lot at home . . . and, if we don't have the ¼ cup, we have to combine two other fractions cups together to make ¼. So, if you're outside and you look around, math is everywhere. There's numbers all over the place and fractions and percents and everything. Math is something you have to deal with [be]cause math is all over the place. I think it's important to learn [be]cause wherever you look, there's math.[11]

This one example suggests that emphasizing high cognitive demand tasks support Black girls' mathematics development, because these tasks require something different of Black girls—to make connections, analyze information, and draw conclusions.[12]

Each curriculum contained regular routines, but they varied in length, when they were to be used, and focus. Routines are the daily teacher-students-content interactions and are important to examine because they embody the rules of engagement of teaching and learning.[13] Routines communicate expectations and norms for students; therefore, understanding the routines' focus can shed light on the extent to which students succeed at high-quality academic work. For example, *Saxon* devoted twenty minutes per day to routines that included six to nine daily fluency activities, such as reading calendars and clocks, counting, and graphing the weather and attendance. *Investigations*, on the other hand, included ten minutes per day and included one activity identified from a set of four conceptually oriented activities focused on number relationships and time. *SFAW* did not include a specified regular routine but provided a problem of the day and practice worksheet. Finally, the different curricula used repeated practice to reinforce the concepts taught in the lesson. In *Saxon*, repeated practice of the new skill was incorporated in each daily lesson and focused on fluency of facts; students could also work on their basic mathematics facts or number concepts prior to the lesson or at a different time of the day. In comparison, *Expressions* placed minimal emphasis on repeated practice within the lesson but did provide follow-up worksheets to reinforce the content of the lesson. Understanding Black girls' perspectives of repeated practice and routines for learning mathematics is a line of inquiry that has not been studied extensively, but we do know that repeated practice for the memorization of facts invokes fear and anxiety.[14]

While research shows that knowledge of math facts is important, mathematics educator Clifton Boaler points out that the best way for students to know math facts is by using them regularly and developing an understanding of numerical relations—memorization, speed, and test pressure can be damaging.[15] We also know that instructional routines should be used to support Black girls' development of the five strands of mathematical proficiency (conceptual understanding, procedural fluency, strategic competence, adaptive reasoning, and productive disposition) suggested by the National Academies of Sciences, Engineering, and Medicine and the eight standards for mathematics practice as described by the Common Core State Standards (make sense of problems and persevere in solving them, reason abstractly/quantitatively, construct viable arguments/critique the reasoning of others, model with mathematics, use appropriate tools strategically, attend to precision, look for and make use of structure, and look for and express regularity in repeated reasoning).[16] Instructional routines in mathematics curricula should be clearly defined routines for interactions and discourse that support Black girls' engagement in mathematical practices and their learning of mathematics content. This is especially important for Black girls because teachers spend too much time focusing on keeping them quiet, rather than giving them a big voice for developing into strong mathematicians.[17]

Instructional approach was the second area these scholars compared across the four curricula. Instructional approach can be broken down into three related categories: (a) the intended instructional model, (b) the expected teacher role during instruction, and (c) the nature of the classroom interactions. The instructional model is usually characterized in one of two ways—direct instruction or "ambitious instruction."[18] Just as it sounds, with direct instruction, the teacher directs the learning. She is positioned as the authority and source of knowledge, along with the mathematics textbook. Her role is to establish how, what, and when the students learn; she transmits knowledge to the students and manages their processing and uptake of ideas. Freire called direct instruction "banking education"—all teachers do is deposit knowledge into the heads of the students because they are viewed as empty vessels.[19] Ambitious instruction, on the other hand, values student generation of knowledge, establishes instructional pathways to foster this generation, and allows students to share their knowledge with others. Remillard and colleagues characterized the teacher's role and the nature of classroom interactions as the teacher and student behaviors necessary for achieving the intended instructional model. The teacher's role focuses specifically on what she typically does during a lesson—modeling or showing, explaining, guiding, and facilitating. Classroom interactions refer to the primary types of interactions designed in the curriculum plans, such as with who or what students interact: the mathematics textbook, the teacher, or other students.

Remillard and colleagues found that *Investigations* was the only curriculum that focused on ambitious instruction, facilitated student production of ideas, and structured different interactions, such as teacher-student and student-student. *Saxon* and *SFAW* used direct instruction models, whereby the teacher explained, guided, and demonstrated most of the mathematics lessons, and the students only interacted with the text. *Expressions* had a blend of both. Because many Black girls are enrolled in primary and secondary public schools that often have limited resources and underqualified mathematics teachers, they are more likely to experience direct instruction models in their mathematics courses, including doing worksheets and the teacher doing all the talking.[20] Therefore, teachers who desire to support Black girls' mathematical development should use ambitious instruction because it can push against deficit narratives about their abilities, shift their perspectives toward positive attitudes about mathematics, and positively influence their mathematics identities.

Support for the teachers embedded in the curriculum guides was the last area compared across the four curricula. Research has shown that teachers are the most critical variable in the implementation of curriculum material designs, and teachers' use of materials can vary significantly.[21] Remillard and colleagues analyzed both how each curriculum provided guidance to teachers and what the guidance communicated. Most conventional teachers' guides or manuals tell the teacher which tasks to give to the students and what questions to ask (called explicit scripts), while other progressive guides go deeper to speak to the teacher about the design of the lesson, the mathematical and pedagogical thinking underlying the lesson, and how the students might respond (called descriptive scripts).[22] Remillard and colleagues found that three of the curricula (*Investigations, Expressions,* and *Saxon*) provided substantial support for the teacher in the form of extensive guidance on how to enact the lessons. *Saxon*'s approach to guiding teachers was mostly explicit in that each lesson in the teacher's guide consists of a fully scripted lesson containing everything the teacher should say and a detailed description of the teacher's intended actions and classroom arrangements. The goal of explicit scripts is to leave nothing to chance by the teacher. Explicit scripts are usually connected to direct instruction models; such a mathematics curriculum is not beneficial for any student learning mathematics concepts.

However, in addition to mathematics curricula of this type not having any faith in teachers' abilities to teach well (and sometimes this is warranted), it also communicates messages to Black girls that a mathematics curriculum focused on deeper thinking through inquiry-based experiences and problem solving is not for them. While we know this is a myth, when Black girls' perceptions of these messages are internalized, especially girls who may not have traditional capital valued in schools and mathematics classrooms specifically, it makes it difficult for them to find their agency and resistance.[23] Overall, Remillard and colleagues' contribution offers useful analytical categories to examine students' opportunities to learn embedded in curricular materials. Their framework helps the field on multiple levels, including curriculum designers, curriculum adoption committees, and other stakeholders with interests in educational equity understand what is important for improving Black girls' opportunities to learn and outcomes.

HIDDEN POWER RELATIONS IN THE ADOPTION OF MATHEMATICS CURRICULA—WHO DECIDES?

As you can see, a curriculum is important for students' mathematical learning; therefore, a school, district, or state's adoption decisions are highly consequential. Every state in the United States has the responsibility of adopting mathematics textbooks. Most states utilize a "state adoption" policy, which means that the state board provides a list of approved mathematics textbooks and establishes a timeline for adoption. But some states have "open-territory" policies, whereby the state does not restrict the choice of textbooks, and decisions about funding and timing of adoptions are made locally, at the district or school level.[24] Whether their policies are state guided or open territory, there appear to be four different types of approaches to adopting mathematics curricula that states use including committee-guided, teacher-driven, administrator-led, and informal.[25] The *committee-guided approach* is composed of mainly teachers who serve as the primary decision-making body in the textbook selection process. That committee works closely with a curriculum leader to choose new mathematics materials. The *teacher-driven model* strives to make the process fair, open, and transparent to teachers. This model protects teachers' participation in the process, and the curriculum director takes a neutral role. To reduce "biases," districts can include processes such as obligating the teachers to hold open and public meetings. The *administrator-led format* includes one administrator who researches the various options to inform and educate the staff about the research. Once that is complete, approved mathematics textbooks options are presented to a committee of teachers. Last, the *informal approach* to mathematics curriculum adoption is usually found in small districts. This approach generally has no official committee appointed and, in some cases, no specific criteria for assessing the mathematics textbooks.[26]

These approaches make it clear *who* makes decisions for mathematics curriculum adoption—teachers, curriculum directors, administrators. These individuals hold much power and are more than likely white and middle class. Federal data show that more than 80 percent of the public and private elementary and secondary school teachers are white, making white teachers overrepresented in the teaching force.[27] We can assume then that Black teachers are seldom afforded the same opportunities to participate in mathematics curriculum adoption processes, since they represent only 6 percent of the teaching profession.[28] Their voices and perspectives are absent in these major decisions. This is not to say that all Black teachers are critically aware and would bring a critical perspective; this is to point out that white values and interests dominate in this process. But even for some of the Black teachers in public and private schools, prior research overwhelmingly shows that they are rarely positioned as content experts, but are instead viewed as incompetent, disciplinarians, role models, and othermothers, so their likelihood of being appointed to these mathematics curriculum committees remains limited.[29] Overall, curriculum adoption committees take a variety of approaches to adopting mathematics curriculum, and those committees are often void of critical perspectives that can problematize how Black girls are erased in mathematics curricula processes.

When these curriculum leaders come together to examine different mathematics curricula for adoption, they often have three goals. The first goal is a focus on "fit" for their mathematics programs. A few things inform this notion of fit including the students' summative assessment data, how aligned the curriculum is to their state's standards or the national Common Core State Standards for Mathematics (CCSSM), quality, or results from pilot-testing research.[30] One organization that districts may look to in determining quality is EdReports. EdReports.org is an independent nonprofit designed to improve education by providing free reviews of K–12 instructional materials. It uses a rubric that supports the review process through what it calls three gateways. The mathematics curricula materials reflect the importance of alignment to college- and career-ready standards and other attributes of high-quality curriculum, such as usability and design. Mathematics curricula are reviewed through gateway one—focus and coherence—because the CCSSM calls for a narrowing and deepening of topics so that students have strong foundations of mathematics concepts. This is different from what US mathematics curricula typically do, which is superficially cover many topics, described as a "mile wide and an inch deep," leaving students with shallow understandings of mathematical concepts.[31]

Coherence emphasizes linking topics and thinking across grades. We often hear people say that mathematical ideas are like building blocks, and this is true for how it is constructed in our current scope and sequence. For example, students need a strong foundation in number sense, whole numbers, operations, and solving problems involving these ideas before they are ready to learn fractions because there are cognitive obstacles that can occur for students when the operations using fractions do something different from operations using whole numbers.[32] Multiplying whole numbers produces a larger number, but multiplying fractions gives a smaller number. Often, students struggle to understand why multiplication works differently with different numbers, especially if the instruction they receive concentrates on procedures without connections.

Mathematics curricula are reviewed on gateway two—rigor and use of the eight mathematical practices. CCSSM defines rigor as having three aspects: conceptual understanding, procedure skills and fluency, and application. Rigor does not mean introducing topics in earlier grades. It means that students have a deep and authentic command of mathematical concepts such that they see mathematics as more than a set of discrete procedures, calculate with accuracy, and correctly apply mathematical knowledge to solve problems.

Gateway three focuses on the question of usability. Are the instructional materials user-friendly for students and educators? Materials must be well designed to facilitate student learning and enhance a teacher's ability to differentiate and build knowledge within the classroom. These gateways are important, and the reports created using this rubric can empower districts and increase the capacity of teachers, administrators, and leaders to seek and identify the highest-quality instructional materials. The reports are viewed as comprehensive, and they are informed by evidence-based research. All in all, "fit" as a goal for mathematics curriculum adoption is complex because while alignment of mathematics curricula to state standards is important, the various mathematics curricula designs are not informed by evidence-based research involving Black girls. There is a dire need for empirical research that clarifies how mathematics curricula can enable discretionary space and pathways for Black girlhood liberation.

The second goal that curriculum leaders focus on when adopting mathematics instructional materials is to build teachers' commitment to using the textbooks. Teachers play a substantial role in shaping the mathematics curriculum experienced by students; thus, if they do not find materials appealing, implementation suffers.[33] There are several early studies that showed many teachers struggle to understand new mathematics materials, noting a clash between their beliefs about mathematics and the ideals represented in the materials.[34] In her study that compared teachers' uses of topics, student pages, and teacher suggestions, Susan Stodolsky found that teachers consistently adhered to the topics in their textbooks but departed from many accompanying teaching suggestions.[35] But even more recent studies continue to show the tensions between written mathematics curriculum and teachers' enactment of that written curriculum.[36] Some scholars have pushed even further to consider mathematics teachers' enactment of particular CCSSM reform strategies.[37] Using multilevel regression models based on data collected from 288 secondary student surveys and 33 mathematics teachers' classrooms observations in 16 different schools, Charles Munter and Cara Haines found that students of color were more likely to perceive racial differences in opportunity than were white students, and those differences were amplified in classrooms where teachers were observed attempting high-level mathematical tasks but failing to maintain the cognitive demand of those tasks throughout the lesson.[38] These studies underscore the complexities and power relations involved in curriculum adoption processes.

Earlier, I argued that certain curricula emphasized more conceptual understanding and connections than others. Knowing that some teachers struggle with implementing reform-oriented mathematics curricula, they may acquiesce to what is easy rather than what is right and just; teachers often do not know how to use these curricula, so they go with what they know, even though their decisions perpetuate harm to Black girls. Thus, when we think through Black girl cartography, we see that because of many Black girls' experiences in mathematics classrooms with teachers who already deem many of them as problems and more social than academic, curriculum adoption processes become more consequential for marginalized students.

The third goal is to ensure that the process is fair and transparent. Districts aim to protect against biases and corruption by seeking input from a range of stakeholders, considering multiple options, establishing criteria for evaluating textbooks on their merit, and looking for independent data as evidence of quality.[39] This process appears democratic, but can be problematized when considering the adoption processes of NSF-funded mathematics curricula in the early 2000s, long before adoption frameworks around fit and teacher commitment were deployed.[40] If districts wanted to adopt the research-based mathematics curricula, the developers of the curriculum materials required the accompanied professional development for the teachers. It was a requirement because it became clear that many teachers were unable to implement the programs in the spirit that the authors intended. This made the price tag increase significantly, making it a nonstarter for districts that could not afford to buy the materials and train the teachers. As a result, the adoption process can fall short of fair aims; consequently, Black girls' learning needs continue to go unmet. Nothing about the adoption process is fair and transparent.

THE POLITICS OF OFFICIAL MATHEMATICS KNOWLEDGE AND TEACHER ENACTMENT

The curricula that the state, district, and school adopt become the official mathematics knowledge that every student needs to know and be able to do. While this process can unfold in different ways, overall, it is insulated from critical perspectives that challenge the Eurocentric focus many mainstream mathematics curricula underscore. The prominence of white values and interests reflected through mathematics curricula is not always explicit but, instead, often hidden from everyday view. For example, we learned that curriculum adoption committees' goals depend on whether the leaders see a "fit" for their mathematics program, whether teachers like the curricula, and whether the process is (ostensibly) democratic, but these three goals ultimately serve the status quo of educators' comfort and habit. They also rest on a deeply flawed mathematics education system that has infrequently served Black girls equitably. Thus, when mainstream mathematics curricula meet liberation-informed mathematics agendas centering Black girl joy, for example, collisions can occur. Mathematics curricula and enactment become a space of contestation and politics, because the standardization of a mathematics curriculum comes up short when freedom is the aim for Black girls' learning of mathematics.

To push back on the status quo embodied in mathematics curricula, educators sometimes resort to teacher-created materials. However, the status quo does not only reside in published textbooks. Teachers' understanding of mathematics curriculum enactment from a broader socio-political perspective is critical. For the last several years, a deluge of news reporting shows inappropriate mathematics curricula across the United States. For example, teachers in large states such as New York, California, and Georgia used mathematics problems with themes of slavery (i.e., whippings, auctions). The following are examples of the mathematics problems that teachers constructed, shared with other teachers, and sent home with elementary school students. Following each problem is a possible Common State Standard the teachers aimed to teach.

In a slave ship, there can be 3,799 slaves. One day, the slaves took over the ship. 1,897 are dead. How many slaves are alive?[41] *(Represent and solve problems involving addition and subtraction)*

One slave got whipped five times a day. How many times did he get whipped in a month (31 days)? Another slave got whipped nine times a day. How many times did he get whipped in a month? How many times did the two slaves get whipped together in one month?[42] *(Use the four operations with whole numbers to solve problems)*

A plantation owner had 100 slaves. If three-fifths of them are counted for representation, how many slaves will be counted?[43] *(Represent and solve problems involving the four operations with fractions)*

Each tree has 56 oranges. If eight slaves pick them equally, then how much would each slave pick?[44] *(Represent and solve problems involving division and multiplication)*

If Frederick got two beatings each day, how many beatings did he get in one week?[45] *(Represent and solve problems involving repeated addition)*

Frederick had six baskets filled with cotton. If each basket held five pounds, how many pounds did he have all together?[46] *(Represent and solve problems involving multiplication of whole numbers)*

The master needed 192 slaves to work on a plantation in the cotton fields. The fields could fill 75 bags of cotton. Only 96 slaves were able to pick cotton for that day. The missus needed them in the Big House to prepare for the Annual Picnic. How many more slaves are needed in the cotton fields?[47] *(Represent and solve problems involving addition and subtraction of whole numbers)*

These questions are horrific. To be clear, while these slavery-themed mathematics problems were not likely found in a mainstream mathematics textbook or teachers' manual, they were designed by teachers aiming to teach mathematics standards and also represent an epistemological fatality when educational leaders, including teachers, curriculum developers, administrators, instructional mathematics coaches, and other decision-makers think that mathematics is apolitical, universal, and just a tool for doing calculations. Margaret Hartmann, author of one of the many news stories about the New York City teachers published in 2013 in the *New York Intelligencer*, stated:

So, there were actually two teachers who didn't think it was inappropriate to have kids work on math problems that casually reference people suffering and dying with little historical context. But how were they supposed to know? It's not like there was a highly publicized story about a teacher getting in trouble for the exact same thing just a year ago.[48]

Hartmann referenced the news story about Luis Rivera, a third-grade teacher at Beaver Ridge Elementary School in Gwinnett Country, Georgia, who also sent home math homework that asked questions about slavery and beatings the year before in 2012. The Georgia district spokesperson, Sloan Roach, highlighted that several teachers were trying to do a cross-curricular activity between social studies and mathematics. Others suggested that the teachers were just racist, and they should be fired. Despite these "bad apple" protestations, the larger racial project of mathematics curricula needs to be recognized: the preservation of a hegemonic structural system in mathematics knowledge that is taken for granted.

Integrating mathematics into social studies is a powerful instructional practice; however, absent a deep understanding of how mathematics is used as a tool for oppression, both historically and today, it cannot be done well and in humanizing ways.[49] The deep understanding comes from critical reflection and praxis—what Freire called *conscientization*.[50] Mathematics curriculum designers, teachers, and other educators need to develop a critical awareness of personal, social, economic, and political realities of African American students and communities in the United States to decrease the development and use of dehumanizing mathematical tasks constructed by teachers enacting state mathematics curricula standards. It is difficult to conceive that the latest Los Angeles case at Windsor Hills Elementary School happened only five years ago in 2017.[51]

MATHEMATICS CURRICULA IN SOLIDARITY WITH THE LIBERATION OF BLACK GIRLS

In this chapter, I have argued that mainstream mathematics curricula design, adoption, and enactment are processes that render Black girls' liberatory mathematics education invisible by school structures and the omission of critical perspectives. These school structures and omissions implicitly and explicitly promote the preservations of white values and interests. Therefore, I present a sample mathematics curriculum that demonstrates a vision for how to design a curriculum that can transform personal, social, economic, and political structures for many Black girls' liberation, now and over time. I am aware that the implementation of such a Black girl–centered mathematics curriculum into the mainstream is a tall order; however, informal spaces (e.g., afterschool and summer programs, homeschoolers) are more likely to engage in this radical and epistemic social movement project.

The curriculum is informed by the frameworks discussed in the introduction—*endarkened feminist epistemology, critical race theory, intersectionality,* and *Black feminism.* It is centered on the research, study, and development of Black girls and women as emerging and actualized mathematicians.[52] Designing mathematics curricula in these ways is critical, because we want all Black girls to thrive and see themselves (or some version of themselves) across an intergenerational group of Black girls and women in mathematics. This vision increases their self-awareness about the power of mathematics as a discipline to learn and use for (1) addressing injustices Black girls care about, and (2) creating, innovating, and social engineering their personal and professional dreams. Thus, this curriculum is not about learning mathematics concepts to pass a course or get a good grade, but it is about contributing to what Alston called an urban mathematics renaissance (see chapter 2). The poem "The Dream Keeper" by Langston Hughes speaks to the importance of Black girls' dreams being realized, and I would argue that mathematics can play a role in bringing Black girls' dreams to fruition. Hughes writes:

Bring me all of your dreams,
You dreamers,
Bring me all of your
Heart melodies
That I may wrap them
In a blue cloud-cloth
Away from the too-rough fingers
Of the world[53]

Black girls and women have heart melodies—their ideas and goals for better lives—but many of their dreams are crushed by mathematics teachers and educators generally who simply do not believe in them. Their dreams are also crushed through the amplification of broader racialized and gendered societal norms and stereotypes about their intersectional identities and their mathematics abilities. This curriculum unit aims to disrupt these challenges.

I am inspired by the work of Tiffany Nyachae, who developed, along with other Black women teachers, the Sisters of Promise (SOP) curriculum for fifth- through eighth-grade Black girls.[54] Across an academic school year, eighty Black girls engaged in activities and tools: weekly afterschool classes, one-to-one academic reflections and planning, parent activities, a camping trip, and an end-of-year gala in order to be empowered academically, intellectually, socially, emotionally, and physically.[55] The mission of SOP is for the girls to become future leaders in their communities. SOP has seven core values, five of which are useful in this discussion—*sisterhood, leadership, self-awareness, financial literacy,* and *effective communication.*[56] I use these five values to develop a mathematics curriculum unit that focuses on exploring data science through the lives, scholarship, and activism of Black women and girls. This is not a traditional unit in data science concepts, but instead emphasizes Black girls' development of these values. *Sisterhood* is about developing a strong bond with other girls in order to support each other in achieving similar goals. *Leadership* is developing the ability to set high standards and act positively so that others will want to follow, with the understanding that the role of humility, co-constructing of knowledge, and different levels of feedback are central to excellent leadership. *Self-awareness* refers to the girls having a consciousness of self in terms of who they are and their purpose in relation to the world. Rather than *financial literacy,* I use mathematics literacy broadly to focus on the girls' capacity to formulate, employ, and interpret mathematics in a variety of contexts. *Effective communication* is articulating data and findings in clear ways on posters (they will create and present at the end of the unit) as well as speaking with authority and confidence that commands respect for themselves and others, all while being a good listener.

This three-week unit is designed for fifth- through eighth-grade Black girls but could be adapted in any way for younger or older Black girls. Additionally, while this unit is designed to speak specifically to Black girls, it could be used with any group of students, because it disrupts dominance in how to learn mathematics topics and concepts; all students benefit from such experiences.

UNIT TITLE: Exploring Data Science Through the Lives, Scholarship, and Activism of Historical and Contemporary Black Women and Girls

UNIT SUMMARY: This unit uses the lives, scholarship, and activism of Black women and girl leaders from the United States and around the world to explore basic data science concepts. Data science is the study of data. It involves developing methods of recording, storing, and analyzing data to effectively extract useful information. In this unit, students read archival documents, essays, articles, social media outlets (blogs), and listen to podcasts to mine various primary and secondary sources to better understand their chosen Black woman or girl, how these women used data in their work/lives, and make connections to the core values of leadership, self-awareness, sisterhood, mathematics literacy, and effective communication. The Black women and girls can be famous or not. For example, if a student's cousin is an activist or social entrepreneur and that student wants to use them for their project, it is permitted.

RELEVANCE TO LIVES/FUTURES: Organizations such as schools, grocery stores, social media platforms (i.e., Instagram), hair salons, churches, airlines, and community centers routinely look for new ways to capture and learn from data. Data are everywhere, and everyday people use data—both informal and formal data—to make decisions; examples include the quickest drive to work, the best day and time to host a Christmas party, can a family afford for their children to be in the school band, challenge to a dress code school policy, and ways that Walmart's Lysol and toilet paper inventories changed as a result of the COVID-19 global pandemic. Knowing and understanding how to use data is a critical skill in today's society, so access to the data science field is important for all individuals, whether they want to be an accountant, trade worker (i.e., builder, plumber, electrician), dentist, teacher, or self-employed business owner. Black girls will reason with, and think critically about, data in all forms.

FORMATIVE ASSESSMENTS:

1. Exploration document (who, what, when, where, and why)
2. Problem statement (what is the problem that your Black woman/girl is trying to solve?)
3. Significance statement (why was/is their work important? How did/do they use data to help them address the problem that they care about?)
4. Research questions (what kinds of questions did your Black woman/girl ask while doing their work? What questions do you want to explore more?)
5. Methods statement (describe how you went about doing your research of your chosen Black woman or girl)
6. Theory statement (explain what you think drives or makes your Black woman or girl do the work they do?)
7. Research text messages, blogs, memos (what are some things that you notice or wonder about as you are doing your exploration?)
8. Interview protocol (come up with questions for your interview with your Black woman/girl—you may or may not get to actually interview them, but what would you want to ask if you are trying to understand data science concepts?)
9. Poster draft (put together the "story" you want to tell using a presentation software, such as Prezi, PowerPoint, or Publisher)
10. Reference list document (organize the sources that you used to explore your Black woman or girl—magazine articles, YouTube videos, social media posts, books, etc.)

SUMMATIVE ASSESSMENT: Research poster to be shared at an exhibition. Audience includes community members, parents, family, teachers, general educators, and professional Black women data scientists to provide feedback to the girls. This requires prework of identifying willing professional Black women who work in data science or other professions that use mathematics. Locating five would make a great panel of judges.

POSSIBLE BLACK WOMEN AND GIRLS TO EXPLORE:

1. Joy Buolamwini started the Algorithmic Justice League to fight against racial and gender biases in artificial intelligence or AI services offered from companies like Amazon or Microsoft.
2. Dr. Kizzmekia (Kezzy) Corbett is a National Institutes of Health scientist who supported the development of the vaccine for COVID-19.
3. Marley Dias founded #1000blackgirlbooks when she was thirteen.
4. Dr. Latanya Sweeney studies discrimination (treating people unfairly because of race, gender, or other identity) in social media.
5. Ida B. Wells (1862–1931) was a journalist and activist who worked to create and pass antilynching laws for Black people.
6. India Skinner, Mikayla Sharrieff, and Bria Snell, Banneker High School students in Washington, DC, created a filtration system when they were in the eleventh grade because the water in the fountains in their high schools was contaminated.
7. Aja Owens and Adrienne Draper are sisters who publish books that affirm Black girls.
8. Brittany Rhodes is a mathematician and tech founder of *Black Girl MATHgic*.
9. Dr. Jedidah Isler is an astrophysics and host of online platform *Vanguard: Conversations with Women of Color in STEM*.
10. Yeshimabeit (Yeshi) Milner is cofounder and executive director of Data for Black Lives.

NATIONAL STANDARDS:

Grade 5: Represent and interpret data (Common Core Standards Mathematics)

Grades 6–8: Develop and use models to represent data (Next Generation Science Standards)

Grades 6–8: Analyze and interpret data (Next Generation Science Standards)

Grades 6–8: Engage in argument from evidence (Next Generation Science Standards)

Grades 6–8: Examine personal identity and how it is shaped by culture, groups, and institutions (National Council for the Social Studies)

Grades 6–8: Develop civic competence through political thought and various structures of power (National Council for the Social Studies)

Grades 6–8: Learn how to apply civic ideas in action to exercise democratic freedom and the pursuit of the common good (National Council for the Social Studies)

Grades 6–8: Read informational texts—key ideas/details, integrate knowledge and ideas, cite textual evidence (Common Core Standards Literacy)

Grades 6–8: Write informative/explanatory texts to examine a topic and convey ideas and information clearly (Common Core Standards Writing)

Grades 6–8: Engage effectively in a range of collaborative discussion: one-on-one, small groups and teacher-led (Common Core Standards Speaking/Listening)

Grades 6–8: Present claims and findings, emphasizing salient points in a focused, coherent manner with relevant evidence, sound valid reasoning, and well-chosen details; use appropriate eye contact, adequate volume, and clear pronunciation (Common Core Standards Speaking/Listening)

Tables 3.1 and 3.2 include Monday-through-Friday schedules for weeks 1 and 2. Each day has *Essential Question(s)*, *Core Values*, *Launch and Explore*, *Journal Writing*, and *Share Out*.

WEEK #1 SAMPLE LESSONS:

Materials: Mathematics journals

Vocabulary: Each girl will decide what vocabulary she needs to better understand. Terms will be identified in their journals.

WEEK #2 SAMPLE LESSONS: Lots of independent, small group, and one-to-one teacher activity this week. Girls will do work, get feedback, revise, get

TABLE 3.1 Sample lessons for week 1

MONDAY	TUESDAY	WEDNESDAY	THURSDAY	FRIDAY
Essential questions: Who am I in mathematics?	**Essential questions:** What do data say about Black girls and math? What are my interpretations of these data? What do I think about these data? Learning about this makes me want to ask other questions, such as _____.	**Essential questions:** Where can I find Black girls doing math? How does this make me feel? What do I wonder about?	**Essential questions:** What is data science? How can it be explored through the lives of Black girls/women?	**Essential questions:** Which Black girl or woman do I want to explore to learn more about how they used data in their lives?
Core value: self-awareness	**Core values:** self-awareness, math literacy, sisterhood, effective communication, and leadership	**Core values:** sisterhood, leadership, effective communication, math literacy	**Core values:** mathematics literacy, effective communication	**Core values:** sisterhood, effective communication
Launch/Explore	*Launch/Explore*	*Launch/Explore*	*Launch/Explore*	*Launch/Explore*
Whole class: Discussion about their biographies in learning mathematics from K–present.	**Partners:** Go online and Google "Black girls and math." Share findings with whole group. Ask the girls to identify "patterns" they see from what we have found as a collective. Record these patterns on the chart paper.	**Guest panel:** High school and college Black girls who are enrolled in advanced math courses and majoring in math or math-based science or engineering.	**Teacher mini interactive lecture:** What is data science? Teacher asks the girls questions about what they already know about data and how they use data personally as well as how professionals might use data.	Teacher does a "Black girl/woman talk" of the 10 girls/women identified. This is to give a quick glimpse to peak the girls' interests.
Journal: Write a 2-page mathematics autobiography responding to questions such as: What is my earliest memory of doing math? Was it with my family, friends, school? When was the last time I enjoyed math? What was it about that time that made it fun or interesting? What do I most love about math? What do I dislike about math? What advice would you give your little sister about learning math? What advice would you give your future math teacher about how you like to learn math?	**Journal:** Based on what we learned together, write a paragraph about why you think there are so few Black girls taking advanced math courses in middle, high school, or college? What would be your plan to improve this?	Girls listen and engage with these young women. Girls will develop questions to ask the panel beforehand so conversation started. **Small group:** Each guest panelist will spend time with a small group of girls to just talk and ask follow-up questions about their lives, math, or whatever they want. **Journal:** What did you learn today from our panelists? Are you experiencing any emotions? If so, what are they and why do you think you feel a way?	**Partners:** Go online to explore how people use data in their lives and in their jobs or professions. Girls report back, and we detail our collective learning to look for patterns. Teacher creates a working chart of the patterns that gets posted for their use at any time they need reminders. **Journal:** What do you now know about data science that you did not know before? Do you think data are useful? Why? What type of data do you think you might want to collect one day for fun?	**Partners or individual:** Go online and search your Black woman and girl. **Library:** Take the girls to the local library to research their Black women or girl. **Journal:** Who did you choose to learn more about? Why? State the who, what, when, where, and why. Share out!
Share out!	Share out!	Share out!	Share out!	

TABLE 3.2 Sample lessons for week 2

MONDAY	TUESDAY	WEDNESDAY	THURSDAY	FRIDAY
Essential questions: Problem statement (what is the problem that your Black woman or girl is trying to solve?), and significance statement (why was their work important? How did they use data to help them address the problem that they cared about?) Core values: self-awareness, math literacy, effective communication	**Essential questions:** Research questions (what kinds of questions did your Black woman or girl ask while doing their work?) Methods statement (describe how you went about doing your research of your chosen Black woman or girl). Core values: self-awareness, math literacy, sisterhood, effective communication, leadership	**Essential questions:** Theory statement (explain what you think drives or makes your Black woman or girl do the work they do?) Core values: sisterhood, leadership, effective communication, math literacy	**Essential questions:** What is an interview protocol? Core value: effective communication	**Essential questions:** What is a research poster? How does it communicate all the work that you did in your study? Core values: effective communication, sisterhood
Launch/Explore Girls answer these questions independently based on their research. Some may have to go back online to find additional information. Later, we do a "critical friends"** circle where the girls will present their problem statements for feedback.	*Launch/Explore* **Teacher:** Short video on primary and secondary sources. Critical friends groups of the girls' responses to the questions from the day before. There could be a need for a mini lecture on the spot to discuss more about methods.	*Launch/Explore* **Teacher:** Mini interactive lecture on "theory." Use lots of examples of how we come to explain things. What do we take into consideration? For example, how do we explain why our siblings or friends "annoy us"? Teacher should discuss that theory explains phenomena, such as why we get nervous about a test or why our parents or guardians try to protect us from danger.	*Launch/Explore* **Whole group discussion:** Have you ever interviewed someone? What was it like? What kinds of questions did you ask? What did you learn from the interview? **Partners:** Identify 5 questions that you would ask your Black woman or girl if you could. Go online to see if you can find their email or contact information. Craft an email message or letter together asking them your 5 questions. They may not respond, and that is OK.	*Launch/Explore* Teacher shows several examples of research posters and holds a whole class discussion about what they are and what they do. **Small groups:** Each group will get a poster and use a rubric to determine the things they will be assessed on when they give their own presentations: quality of content, neatness, complete with all components (problem, questions, methods, findings, discussion, future questions).

*Critical friends groups are structures for effective feedback and strong support. They are often used with teachers for helping them improve instruction and student learning. I adopt this structure for the girls to receive feedback from their peers. This improves girls' work, but also positions the girls as knowledge producers.

(continues)

TABLE 3.2 Sample lessons for week 2, *continued*

MONDAY	TUESDAY	WEDNESDAY	THURSDAY	FRIDAY
Launch/Explore	*Launch/Explore*	*Launch/Explore*	*Launch/Explore*	*Launch/Explore*
Journal: Write 5–7 sentences that describe the problem statement and why it is important. Who cares? Or who should care? Why? Share out!	**Journal:** What type of sources did you use to learn more about your Black woman or girl? Identify them as primary or secondary sources. What type of challenges did you face when trying to locate information about your Black women or girl? Share out!	**Journal:** You have identified the problem and significance of the work that your Black woman or girl does. Now, think about why they do it and what drives their passion to do the things they do. **Note:** This lesson on theory is basic, and there is no need to go beyond a basic understanding. The girls need to hear the word "theory" and see how it helps them understand their Black woman or girl. Share out!	Critical friends circle of the girls' interview questions to receive feedback. **Journal:** Did you find contact information for your Black woman or girl? Did you change any of your interview questions based on critical friends? If so, how? What question are you most excited about and why? Share out!	**Whole group:** What questions do you have about putting together your poster? **Individual:** Girls work on putting together their draft poster presentations. **Journal:** What is exciting you about for the exhibition? What are you most nervous about? Share out!

more feedback, and start putting together their posters for the exhibition. Teacher reads their individual journals each day to determine what additional support they need to scaffold learning. Girls will feel seen and heard as individuals when teachers make comments of specific praise and areas for growth in their journals.

WEEK #3 SAMPLE LESSONS: On Monday, Tuesday, and Wednesday of week 3, the girls put together their posters. The expectation is that the high-quality posters will be printed at a professional print shop that lays out slides on fabric. Thursday and Friday are the mock presentations in front of an audience of other mathematics teachers and Black girls from the panel. The goal is to receive feedback on ways to improve and learn how to field questions. The girls should do a final journal entry on what they learned about data science through the lives of their Black woman or girl. They should also respond to a question that asks them how they have personally and academically grown as a result of engaging in this curriculum unit. That following Saturday is the exhibition.

CONCLUSION

When mainstream mathematics curricula do not provide discretionary space for Black girls' liberatory experiences in learning mathematics, educators should develop their own. Of course, this work needs to be taken up with a critical eye, a love for Black girls, and a belief in their potential as mathematics learners. This is not a new task for Black people and communities: when we were not allowed to attend white schools, Black people developed their own schools. I urge parents, mathematics teachers, Black girls themselves, and others who care about the mathematics education of Black girls to come together to campaign for change. We should ask Black girls what they want to know and what they need to be liberated. Teaching them about self-awareness of their own mathematics experiences and what those experiences mean in broader contexts can help them answer the question, "What do you want and need to be liberated?" in more robust ways.

Mathematics curricula should inform and empower Black girls about social structures for the purpose of justice and transformation. Learning through herstories of the self and Black women and girls can aid them in developing new interpretations of deficit master narratives that have been created about Black girls' mathematics learning, development, and achievement. Nyachae points out that the full realization of teaching is a form of community work for Black women teachers, but I would say it is community work for anyone who commits to Black girls' health, lives, and well-being. This community work should center Black girls and connect to the legacy of Black women and girls who have come before them: this can be liberating. I want Black girls to be audacious in their life dreams, to maintain high aspirations, and set lofty goals. This puts Black girls on the road to the Black feminist revolution for solidarity in mathematics education.

4

BLACK FEMINIST MATHEMATICS
PEDAGOGIES (BLACKFMP)

A Pedagogical Model Toward Black Girl
Joy and Liberation in Mathematics Education

*Black girlhood is freedom, and Black girls are free. As an organizing
construct, Black girlhood makes possible the affirmation of Black girls'
lives and, if necessary, their liberation. Black girlhood as a spatial
intervention [italics added] is useful for making our daily lives better
and therefore changing the world as we currently know it.*

—RUTH NICOLE BROWN[1]

C hanging mathematics education for Black girl joy—the internal
self-actualization of vibrancy, satisfaction, hope, self-worth, and self-
love—requires that we create space to envision Black girlhood critically
among and with Black girls who are often the "people least guaranteed
to be centered as valuable in collective work and social movements."[2]
Making Black Girls Count in Math Education is a collective work and aims
to participate in the discourse needed for a Black feminist revolution in
mathematics education. We need new ways to construct Black girl identities
and roles in our STEM society through the adoption of an "oppositional
gaze," bell hooks's concept for people in subordinate positions to resist the
dominant images and messages that communicate their devalued status.[3]
Since mathematics education is an organizing enterprise that consistently
communicates to Black girls and women that their status is not valued

nor welcomed, teachers and other educators who dare to invest in educational equity need to adopt the paradigm of Black girlhood as a practice of resistance and wellness in mathematics education that does not collude with white supremacist sentimentalities of missionaries and cannibals.[4]

Adopting Black girlhood as a practice of resistance and wellness in mathematics is necessary to encourage not only a creative curriculum but also *creative pedagogies* that center Black girls' needs. Centering their needs in mathematics teaching and learning is important for their critical awareness and political education, identity development, and positive visioning of themselves. This chapter explores the question, What types of pedagogies do Black girls report valuing for increasing their participation and understanding of mathematical concepts or ideas and overall development in mathematics? Using Black girls' mathematics experiences as a starting point, how might we develop and use creative and humanizing pedagogies to realize their genius, excellence, brilliance, and make it impossible for them to fail?[5] Putting these questions in conversation with the racialized and gendered ethos of mathematics ideologies, systems, and structures is important because many Black girls at certain stages of their lives may be unaware of their internalization of common ideas and understandings that mathematics is neutral and culture free. Their narratives may not make explicit whether they are being influenced or exposed to the stereotypes surrounding racial, gender, and social class issues with learning and understanding mathematics. Thus, through intersectionality methodology, situating Black girls' mathematics narratives within specific social, cultural, and historical contexts is paramount and my epistemological commitment.[6] I present my Black feminist mathematics pedagogies (BlackFMP) model as one way to respond to Black girls' voices advancing more creative pedagogies that can move Black girls toward a more liberatory mathematics education.

HEY BLACK GIRL! WE HEAR YOU! PROMISING PEDAGOGIES

As I discussed in chapter 1, the typology of invisibility for Black girls is pervasive. Black girls not only lack theoretical contributions to their lived experiences in mathematics classrooms and contexts, but are also seldom given the agency to share those experiences, nor has the world cared enough to ask them. Therefore, I elevate Black girls' voices through quotes and excerpts found in the literature. Because of the limited peer-reviewed published work, some quotes come from dissertations, all save one authored by Black women. Elevating dissertations about Black girls' mathematics experiences written by Black women scholars is a political act and spatial intervention. Using these quotes allows the reader to listen to and hear Black girls speak about their various experiences and perspectives in mathematics classrooms and contexts. I include the Black girl pseudonyms the authors used in their investigations to write Black girls into existence, making their standpoints visible and honoring their humanities.

These quotes are from eight research studies and expand across the K–12 trajectory. Various research questions were asked, but my goal was to identify quotes that illuminated the girls' voices in describing their perspectives about their own mathematics learning. In reading the studies, I created themes across the eight studies. Pedagogies that integrate social, relaxing, and rigorous atmospheres are promising for supporting Black girls' positive mathematics development. Black girls also need to be respected, humanized, and cared for through meaningful relationships. Having opportunities to work in small groups, talk to their peers, and explore different mathematics problems are also forms of instruction Black girls said they wanted while learning mathematics.

Social, Relaxing, and Rigorous Atmospheres

Black girls in these studies desired a social and fun atmosphere; thus, teachers should find ways to teach mathematics content that create normative cultures for fun while also doing important mathematics. Fifth-grader Melissa who wants to be a scientist, stated:

> I like the way Ms. C currently teaches mathematics because while she is teaching my class, she puts it sometimes in a funny way and shows examples while being serious. Math is fun! I like learning and talking about math because it makes me look at math with a serious glance because you need math when you grow up.[7]

Melissa understands that having fun in mathematics is important for her, but she also sees that learning mathematics does call for her to be thoughtful at times because being a scientist means she needs to understand mathematics concepts well. Maria, another fifth grader and aspiring teacher who likes learning mathematics and rejects the stereotype that African Americans are not good at mathematics, reported, "Ms. E does funny actions to help us understand how to do a certain problem."[8] When sixth-grader Gabrielle was asked why she attends a Saturday mathematics enrichment program when she could be hanging out with her friends, she highlighted that it is a fun place where she learns essential mathematics:

> Well, I like it because it's fun and although it's not a social group, you get to talk to people about the different relations and stuff with mathematics and other stuff. And you can find that there's always another way to do something. I was really bad at decimals, so Brother Alston taught me another way to do it and it was so much easier because my teacher, she really—it felt like it was overcomplicated to me. Now it's like when Brother Alston showed me this way and I was like—and he was like okay, that's right. So, you do that. And I was like, yeah, because it works better for me the way Brother Alston shows me. It's not overcomplicated and it's fun. Mathematics can be fun. It's one of the subjects that you dread it before you come to his class and then when you get to his class, everything clicks.[9]

Gabrielle's point pushes back on notions of sanitized mathematics classroom expectations where students who are quiet are somehow learning. She also recognizes that there are several pathways to understanding different mathematical ideas, and she is thankful that Brother Alston showed her a different way. Finally, Brittany, a sixth grader who attended a non-magnet school, recounted an engaging pedagogy her former teacher used to help her learn mathematics. Brittany noted, "Our teacher last year was a good teacher. She taught us math with music. She made up a math rap."[10] Brittany's comment suggests that using more culturally responsive pedagogies, such as involving music, is one way to grow Black girls' interest, engagement, and cognitive closeness with mathematics. Last, ninth-grader Monica, who identified as Haitian Black, shared that it is important for mathematics teachers to not yell at her for wrong answers. She described what makes a good mathematics teacher:

> Because, like I said before, you know *he doesn't yell at you for the wrong answer* [italics added]. He yells, you know, if you don't be quiet and he's trying to, like, help people or anything. Like, he's just a really cool teacher. Like, laid back. He tries to help you and sometimes he makes jokes, which kind of, like, makes you feel better and more relaxed. Because you're like, "Oh, you know he's cool and maybe, like, I can even talk to him if I have a problem."¹¹

Monica seeks positive social interactions with her teachers, including basic care and dignity. This had seldom been her experience in previous courses with different teachers. Although teachers engaging in positive social interactions with their students should be a task that any teacher worth their salt would do, research shows that Black girls report negative interactions with their mathematics teachers. Therefore, this type of punitive teacher behavior, when expressed to Black girls, who already face dehumanization in the classroom, can further exacerbate their perceptions of being outsiders in mathematics.

Respect, Humanity, and Relationships

Pedagogies that promote respect, humanity, and relationships with Black girls are promising for increasing their mathematics engagement, learning, and overall development. Jiera, a high-achieving, talkative, and outgoing middle-school student who attended an ethnically and economically diverse public school, spoke about how her mathematics teacher, Ms. Alpin, made her feel reassured that she would not be ridiculed by other students when asking questions. Jiera stated:

> [In Ms. Alpin's class] We felt comfortable. We knew that nobody would laugh if we raised our hand for a question about . . . like if we didn't understand a problem on the board or something. She made it clear that this is not, you know, if you have a question, ask. And, we're not gonna

laugh at anybody . . . If she [Ms. Alpin] wants us to draw something on the board . . . like an equation . . . my hand would be raised to do it.[12]

Jiera's commentary helps us to see that when Black girls believe that they can trust their teacher, and subsequently are invested in performing well, they extend their participation in class to include working with other students and actively adding to the life and action of the classroom environment.[13] Lil Mamma was a high school freshman, enrolled in Algebra I at a small high school that was 98 percent Black.[14] Lil Mamma poignantly detailed a memory of a previous teacher who she appreciated because of that teacher's willingness to go above and beyond to help her when she did not understand certain mathematics concepts:

> And then my only good teacher I had was my fourth-grade teacher where I can actually say I learned math . . . she helped me with anything I had, you know, trouble with; she was always there by my side. We was testin' for like the proficiency test, but like we had like practice tests and if I didn't get something I would go to her and help her, I mean ask her, and she would help me. Like if there was anything I needed help with, or if I needed to stay after school and get help if I didn't understand something, she would stop what she was doing and even if she was at lunch or gettin' ready to go home, she would stop and help me.[15]

What we learn from Lil Mamma's narrative is that it was important for this Black girl to be validated through the relationship she had with her fourth-grade teacher. She connected "actually learning math" not only with the teacher's commitment to explain mathematics in ways Lil Mamma understood, but also because Lil Mamma saw her teacher taking responsibility for ensuring that she was available when Lil Mamma needed support. Last, middle-schooler Sharonda commented on how she was motivated to pay attention to her mathematics teacher because she supported her to learn mathematics. She stated:

> I really pay attention to her [be]cause I know she's helping us. And she even told us that she's strict [be]cause she's trying to help us. So, I'm glad she's my teacher [be]cause I wouldn't want to be on another team.[16]

Sharonda's sentiment about only wanting to be with teachers who are warm demanders aligns with prior research that suggests this pedagogy includes special nurturing for African American students; teachers are caregivers and dedicated to students' needs.[17]

Group Work and Sharing with Peers

Some Black girls enjoy working in groups to share knowledge as well as get help when they do not understand mathematical ideas. Talented and gifted fifth-grade student Beautiful was described by her teacher as an "organized, accomplished, methodological student who has the ability to make solid connections and applications among mathematical concepts."[18] Beautiful favored learning mathematics, "with everyone in the class so if I don't understand, the [other] kids can help me."[19] A high school Black girl, from a different study, participated in a focus group with other Black girls enrolled in advanced mathematics courses. The girls were asked when the last time was that they enjoyed mathematics and why. One shouted with conviction:

> We got taught! Like she went over stuff that we didn't understand. If we needed help, she would like group us up with people that did understand. I liked how—okay. She was organized. I liked organized teachers. Like it wasn't all over the place. Like she always had like a header for like what the lesson was going to be, and she like kept the problems organized. I could tell what was going on. And the fact that she let us talk with our peers to understand what's going on if we don't really get it.[20]

This quote suggests that this Black girl was not taught mathematics in many of her mathematics classes. It also suggests that she has had limited opportunities to talk and share with her peers in mathematics class. Previous research shows that while some Black girls use group work as a space in which they build math competence and recognize themselves or peers as being competent with mathematics, this type of pedagogy infrequently happens in their classrooms.[21] Natasha, an actively engaged middle-school student was characterized by her mathematics teacher as one who takes initiative. Natasha commented on what she liked about working in groups:

> When we work in groups, it's like we work to see what we know and what the other people know . . . and see if we can learn and catch on to what people do. If somebody missed a part and didn't quite understand it, you can explain it.[22]

What we learn about Natasha is that learning from her peers is important because it can foster partnership and teamwork and fill in areas where she needs more support. This can provide Black girls another way of connecting with their peers in the learning environment, an important aspect of belonging.

Autonomy and Exploration

Pedagogies that allow for Black girls to be autonomous, agentic, and exploratory with mathematical concepts are promising. Ashanti, a fifth grader who likes mathematics because it comes easy to her and is an endeavoring attorney, discussed how she preferred that her teacher allow the students to work on problems first without the teacher explaining. Ashanti noted:

> I like to figure out the problems first and have the teacher explain it to me if I need help. She always has to explain it and then if the class gets it wrong, she yells at us and says to us things like, "do you care what your future is going to be like?" And she teaches too fast and then gets mad at us, but it is her fault because she should have took her time.[23]

Ashanti's narrative illuminates that she seldom gets the opportunity to explore math ideas first. This appears to be important to Ashanti because when the teacher instructs on various math concepts first and the class gets it wrong, the teacher is not happy and yells. This narrative also points out that teachers may be teaching at a pace that does not allow Black girls to learn mathematical concepts in a deep way. Research shows that most mathematics teachers teaching in high-poverty urban schools strictly adhere to curriculum pacing guides, prohibiting many students from learning deeply and limiting teachers' creative pedagogies.[24]

An eighth-grade girl who participated in a focus group about what type of instructional strategies happen in their mathematics classrooms, and of those that occur, which ones they like best, provides some insight.[25] One girl referenced working in self-directed groups without the teacher as a pedagogy she liked when she spoke:

> I feel like teachers can't explain it like other people. We are helping each other. Like to show people how to do it my way and for people to say mine is the easiest and everyone starts doing it my way.[26]

What we learn from the quote is that this middle-school girl prefers to work in groups without teacher interference fostering some level of independence. She highlights that peers speak a language that she understands, and she feels confident and competent when her peers like and use strategies she authors. This helps some Black girls feel confident about what they know and demonstrates to the teacher and the class their important mathematical knowledge, signaling self-sufficiency. Black girls viewing themselves as knowledge producers of math ideas is important.

Last, Mane Gurl, a ninth grader who rated herself a nine out of ten for self-efficacy, shared a time when she was proud of herself. She commented:

> My proudest math moment was about four months ago. I was in tutoring and I needed help with a subject on math. I asked my tutoring teacher if she could help me, but she told me the truth and said, "I don't want to lie to you, I don't know how to do it myself." She suggested I go ask someone else who knew about math. But I spotted a book that could help me with my problem. I ended up taking that book home and studying it. I came back to tutoring the next day and I found out how to do the subject I needed help on. I was so happy and glad that for a change I helped myself.[27]

Being independent to solve her issue of not understanding a mathematics idea brought much joy to Mane Gurl. "For a change, I helped myself," suggests that Mane Gurl relied on others, such as teachers and tutors and that reliance potentially suffocated her autonomy to believe in herself and her ability to take ownership of her own mathematics learning. Providing Black girls opportunities to experience the satisfaction one can feel when figuring out mathematics problems on their own can support Black girls' self-perceptions as independent learners in mathematics.

Mathematics for Career and College

Many adolescent Black girls desire to have wonderful careers in areas such as social work, cardiology, dentistry, nursing, and cosmetology.[28] But my research showed that many of them are left alone to learn about these professions, rather than in collaboration with teachers and career counselors in their high schools.[29] The following excerpt was from a group of junior and senior Black girls, enrolled in advanced mathematics at their high school. Four of them were in a focus group and were asked about how they learn about what they want to do after high school. The excerpts are sobering:

> **Moderator:** *"How are you learning about what you might do after school?"*
> **Black Girl:** "Honestly, we have to research. We have to do things that we want to do in life, because here, I don't think they'll help us [inaudible 00:23:38] because all they worry about is dress code. All they worry about is what we're doing, but what we are not doing that's important for us to help us with our careers when we leave this school."
> **Black Girl:** "They want us to be in class, but they're not actually taking the time out to step into the class and see what's going on in there and see why our grades are the way they are."
> **Black Girl:** "Like they're mostly just worried about the parents of [blind school] and not like the academic side, like after—like when I leave school, I have to teach myself different stuff because when I come to school, I don't learn any of this. And when I go to college, I'm going to have to really, really go for it because what they should have been teaching me here, I'll then have to learn again at college in a better way, in a harder way."

Black Girl: "Right now, I feel like *nobody really helps us.* Like we're supposed to have a college readiness teacher, and that's supposed to help
us with like our planning out our lives, I guess. But right now, we
don't have a teacher, so we only get a teacher two days out the week.
So, I feel like nobody really helps us efficiently, I guess."

Moderator: *"Is that the case for everyone?"*

Black Girl: "Yes, for us four. We all are in 11th grade, so when you get to
11th grade you have college readiness in the 12th grade too, because
that's when they do application process and all that. But right now,
we don't have a teacher, so we're just doing study hall besides two
days a week, and it's kind of helpful, but not really, because I believe
that the juniors last year were like farther along than we are. Like we
haven't made a wish list or nothing like that, so—and our—but we
haven't even started on our personal statements."[30]

This exchange points to the plethora of literature on Black girls' schooling
experiences that contends their experiences are racialized and gendered;
that teachers and other school personnel care more about attending to
Black girls' social behaviors and dress code, rather than developing the
academics for their future careers.[31] It is clear that the girls endeavor to
do important work in their futures but are not getting support to develop
these aspirations.

A group of girls enrolled in the general and advanced mathematics
courses and from a different focus group mainly expressed that the math
they are learning now will not be useful in their future careers. In the
following powerful commentary, they share their responses:

Black Girl: "It ain't useful."

Black Girl: "I don't know. I don't know what X has to do with anything. I'm
not going to find the X in the future. I don't know why you're finding
it now."

Black Girl: "I don't get how I'm going to find like GCF [Greatest Common
Factor] in a brain. You know what I mean? Like I don't understand

why we're using this or doing this right now when we're not going to use it in the future.

Black Girl: "I think that the math that's in chemistry, that will be useful in the future for nursing and stuff."

Black Girl: "Well, precalculus won't be really useful, but stuff like we learned before I went to precalculus will be useful for business, but precalculus is not going to—it's not going to help anything, really."

Black Girl: "Honestly, I don't think that calculus is really going to affect me that much in the future, because I'm not going to be worried about that. Like I don't need to do synthetic division on makeup and stuff like that. That doesn't make sense."

Black Girl: "I don't think I need math, like for my [inaudible 00:20:05] today, even though it's real-life math, but it's mostly for like jobs that don't require—like I know—I feel like after middle school, that's when math gets done. I feel like you don't need it anymore after that. Like the math we learn, like eighth grade and below was the math we actually needed for the real world, and now the math we're just learning is like just to learn it."

Black Girl: "I'm in applied math, so in applied math, you do real-world equations. So, the best thing we've been doing, I feel like—it's in general like math in his class is the best math I've ever taken, because I know that I'll actually need it in the future . . . And then people actually do this in the real world. That's like real cool about it."[32]

This point of view among the girls suggests that their secondary teachers may not provide openings for them to think through connections between the mathematics they are learning and potential future careers. However, one girl reflected on her experience in her applied math course, showing teachers what is possible for Black girls' excitement about learning mathematics; when they can see these connections between the mathematics and real people's careers, inspiration can ensue. Overall, what these exchanges illuminate is that many Black girls understand that mathematics is important for their future but are often left on their own to figure out how and in what ways. Teachers should focus on facilitating the translation process to develop a desire to pursue college attendance and future career dispositions.

Essence, a fifth grader in the eMode Saturday mathematics enrichment academy, shared that she thinks "[o]ne reason why I come here is because every time I come here I realize there's one other thing in this world that's related to mathematics."[33] Her teacher, Brother Alston, is consistent in ensuring the girls know various ways mathematics is useful beyond the classroom. This form of instruction can support Black girls in becoming more active in making their own connections between home life and mathematics.

Last, as we know that success in mathematics has far-reaching academic and career implications, Black girls' understanding and use of mathematics is critical to their future achievement. Sixth-grader Haley expressed that learning mathematics is important because people use it every day. She commented:

> We are learning more difficult math now because when you get older, you have to deal with things like . . . they're trying to prepare you for the job you're gonna get in the future. So, they teach you a little bit more than when you're younger. And, then you keep adding on to what you learned in kindergarten. You have to keep adding up . . . Like, I just think that, I like math and you just learn so much every year, it's all different and then when you get in 12th grade it's the end . . . I think math is the most important subject because you use it in everyday life.[34]

Haley understands that learning mathematics is like building blocks—there are concepts one must master before new ones can be learned. Her narrative also suggests she has had positive mathematics experiences because she mentioned that she learns so much math every year. Haley's experience implies that when Black girls have encouraging experiences in mathematics and are able to make connections, they can see how and why math has value beyond school.

Listening and hearing Black girls' viewpoints about their teaching and learning experiences in mathematics contributes to a radical solidarity project.[35] Black girls own their ideas about what it means to learn in mathematics and instructional pedagogies that support their learning. When we silence them in our research, we participate in gendered anti-Black symbolic and epistemological systemic violence.[36] Stated another way, when Black girls' learning needs in mathematics are ignored, researchers and educators perpetuate inequalities and intersectional oppression among Black girls. *Making Black Girls Count in Math Education* is not only about illuminating the problems Black girls face in our mathematics education system, but also innovates radical hope for how to dismantle the inequalities they face. The next section introduces my Black feminist mathematics pedagogies (BlackFMP), one model with potential for supporting the pedagogies Black girls highlighted. BlackFMP facilitates principles for educators' teaching practices through Black girl specificity.[37]

BLACK FEMINIST MATHEMATICS PEDAGOGIES (BLACKFMP) MODEL

BlackFMP is a model for radical hope because it has structure; among its components are mathematics education, history, persistence, critical consciousness, and humanity to name a few. BlackFMP has "cognitive resolve," encouraging planned collective action among mathematics teachers, Black girls, their families, and all other educators and stakeholders invested in their liberation. BlackFMP is receptive of political efficacy and supported by courage and collective Black girl excellence.[38] BlackFMP is more than optimism and resists pessimism because it addresses how Black girls, traditionally stripped of their way of knowing, imagine how to survive and then venture forth to thrive in their mathematics education.[39]

My framework includes four dimensions: *critical consciousness, robust mathematics identities 2.0, academic and social integration,* and *ambitious mathematics instruction* (see figure 4.1). These dimensions are interdependent, and it is not enough to engage in just one, especially if the user's outcomes align with supporting Black girls' limitless possibilities in mathematics. Overall, the framework is designed with Black girlhood as its centripetal force and is a tool for mathematics teachers, general educators, curriculum developers, Black girls and their families, and any

FIGURE 4.1   Joseph's Black feminist mathematics pedagogies (BlackFMP) model

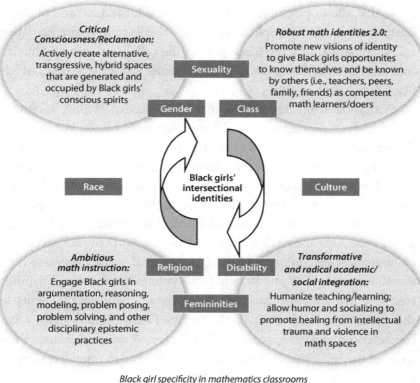

Black girl specificity in mathematics classrooms

other constituency or stakeholder aiming to do liberation work with and on behalf of Black girls.

Critical Consciousness and Reclamation

This dimension is about educators doing the work of developing critical consciousness of Black girlhood in the mathematics classroom and using their power together with Black girls to reclaim the mathematics classroom in new and liberated fashions. This can be achieved in different ways; however, respect, humanity, and relationships with Black girls are structural principles in this dimension. Educators are actively creating alternative, transgressive, and hybrid spaces that are generated and occupied by Black girls' conscious spirits. Conscious spirits gain a language and way of communicating to develop an in-depth understanding of the world that allows for the exposure of social, educational, and political contradictions. For example, asking why schools track in mathematics and why there are so few Black girls in the college-ready mathematics courses are examples of critical-consciousness-raising exercises in which Black girls might engage.

Critical-consciousness development in mathematics must be created outside the regular classroom and in more informal spaces. Mathematics classrooms are killing many Black girls' spirits and their love of learning. In Stephanie Jones's study, the regular mathematics classroom created narrowly defined and oppressive notions of female identities for third-grader Patti.[40] These identities were impossible for Patti to take on successfully because they were rooted in the values of white, middle-class language practices and identities; this ultimately limited Patti's overall success in mathematics. Ms. Smith read Patti as too big, loud, and aggressive, which overshadowed her judgment about Patti's potential and genius. So, Jones created a mathematics club with the purpose of allowing students to show up as their whole and complete selves. Patti's girlhood identity that she practiced at home (raced, gendered, classed) was welcomed in the space of the mathematics club and was used to strengthen her identity in mathematics, often elevating her status among peers.

Critical consciousness is connected to reclamation because when a Black girl becomes conscious about these issues, she has a better opportunity to work in concert with others to act against oppressive elements in her personal life, academic experience, and local and global communities. While working in solidarity with teachers, Black girls reclaim agency, speak out boldly, and empower themselves to make moves toward their liberation. Critical consciousness and reclamation afford Black girls a voice to name inequalities and promote the use of mathematics as a tool for understanding such inequalities, thereby helping them to see the role of mathematics beyond school. This work is critically important because Black girls infrequently see themselves in the mathematics curriculum. Furthermore, this work allows Black girls to reclaim their innocence—to dismantle the adultification they face by educators and society.[41] Research shows that Black girl adultification starts at age five, and when teachers internalize this adultification, they see them as little adults viewed as knowing better when it comes to behaviors. If not addressed, over time adultification can lead some Black girls into the school-to-prison pipeline because teachers do not understand them. So, when mathematics teachers accept these beliefs, they see Black girls as problems in their classroom, not future mathematicians. Educators must work in harmony with Black girls to dismantle these beliefs, perceptions, and ideologies that eclipse Black girl joy. Critical consciousness and reclamation have much potential for disrupting gendered anti-Blackness in important ways. Through these experiences, Black girls see that their social identities are legitimate and have meaning in mathematics contexts. Black girls have an opportunity, through critical-consciousness development and reclamation, to question, critique, analyze, and take action to dismantle negative discursive narratives about their mathematics abilities and achievement.

Robust Mathematics Identities 2.0

A robust mathematics identity can show up in a Black girl when she is given the opportunity to know herself and be known by others (i.e., teachers, peers, family, and friends) as a competent mathematics learner and doer. One way she can know herself as competent is by having many opportunities to autonomously explore mathematical ideas she finds interesting. This can be in relation to mathematical topics or the utility of mathematics in her life, for example, exploring what math she needs to become a doctor. Another way is for her to work in small groups to share what she knows, revise her own thinking, and learn new perspectives from her peers. Professional mathematicians operate in these ways—they make mistakes, they share ideas, and they revise.

Although such learning and participation structures take time to authentically develop to self-actualization, they have the potential to shift socially constructed narratives about who is good and smart at mathematics and what that looks like. Black girls are socialized in our mathematics education system in the same ways as other students, so they may perceive that performing well on mathematics tests, getting good grades, memorizing formulas easily, understanding mathematical concepts without help, and/or answering questions quickly are abilities that someone with a robust mathematics identity would have.[42] Therefore, it is important for Black girls to engage in exploration and small group work to support their mathematics identities development.

I should note that sometimes meta-cognitive conversations with Black girls about how these experiences help push back on smart narratives are critical, especially since they face the stereotypes about Black people (racialized) and girls (gendered) in general not being smart in mathematics. Ebony McGee defined a robust mathematics identity as the strength and agency that college students develop despite their racialization to maintain self-motivated mathematics success.[43] BlackFMP seeks to extend McGee's original conceptualization of a robust mathematics identity to include self-actualization of resistance and critique. Robust mathematics identities 2.0 (RMI 2.0), then, are exemplified by K–12 Black girls who not only understand mathematics concepts deeply and are successful by conventional and nonconventional standards but are also self-actualized in deeply understanding who they are in mathematics. Someone might say, "I identify as a Black girl mathematician," or "I am a Black girl in mathematics." She conceptualizes her own success in mathematics through the rejection of values and ideologies aligned with mainstream ideas. But she cannot do this work alone; it must be in solidarity with her teachers. A Black girl with robust mathematics identities 2.0 knows how to tap into herself and her community to remind herself of why she loves mathematics when the noise and nonsense around her gets too loud.

For many Black girls, this disposition of resistance will take many years, but it is worth our time and labor to support her on this journey to strong and productive mathematics identities. Overall, what RMI 2.0 affords Black girls is a new vision for seeing themselves authentically in mathematics contexts to make independent decisions about how mathematics can be used in the world beyond school. RMI 2.0 disrupts gendered anti-Blackness because it gives Black girls tools to revise old and misguided interpretations and understandings of what a mathematics identity is and who has experiences for developing one.

Academic and Social Integration

BlackFMP promotes the humanization of the learning experience by making the academic social and the social academic—it becomes one space of mind and body. In her seminal text, *Teaching to Transgress*, bell hooks stated:

> Urging all of us to open our minds and hearts so that we can know beyond the boundaries of what is acceptable, so that we can think and rethink, so that we can create new visions, I celebrate teaching that enables transgressions—a movement against and beyond boundaries. It is that movement which makes education the practice of freedom.[44]

I invoke bell hooks because she said educators must overcome a mind-body split, an important construct to explore in mathematics teaching and learning environments. Most mathematics classrooms are serious, and there is no room for play, soulful inquisitiveness, silliness, or being goofy, yet some Black girls desire this type of space to be their full selves and learn mathematics as we learned in their narratives. Humor, for example, humanizes and serves many purposes, including inviting students' broader identities into their learning. Who we are is fundamental to how we make sense of the world; when we must leave parts of our selves at the door in order to be seen as "acceptable," we abandon crucial sensemaking resources. Deep-seated myths and stereotypes about *all* women and girls and about Black people's intellect continue to persist, leaving Black women and girls particularly vulnerable. Furthermore, it is not just that society thinks Black people are mathematically inferior and that women and girls are not smart in mathematics; doing well in mathematics or being recognized as a good mathematics student does not look like being silly, loud, or opinionated. Thus, there is an aspect of Black femininity that gets dismissed, devalued, and dehumanized in mathematics contexts, creating what I call an exponential stereotype.

Stereotypes of Black girlhood get exponentially amplified in the mathematics context when educators continue to internalize these stereotypes over time without critical reflection, disruption, and a commitment to think, to care, and to act in different ways. So, integrating social and academic spaces affords Black girls the freedom and liberation to just be. That is, to be who they are in their fullness, not at the expense of not learning mathematical concepts, but to complement that learning, disrupting gendered anti-Blackness. Integrated spaces as described here also disrupt gendered anti-Blackness because they support healing from intellectual trauma and violence in mathematics contexts.

Ambitious Mathematics Instruction

Ambitious mathematics teaching has become popular in discourse related to mathematics curriculum and pedagogy because it pushes the status quo.[45] Remember that ambitious teaching requires that teachers do two things simultaneously: (1) respond to what students do as they engage in problem solving, and (2) hold students accountable to learning goals that include conceptual understanding, procedural fluency, strategic competence, adaption reasoning, and productive dispositions. These goals are ambitious for sure but do include the assumption that all students get the opportunity to engage in such mathematical practices and learning. What we know is that many Black girls attend low-recourse schools and are generally enrolled in lower-level math classes.[46] As discussed in chapter 3, a mathematics curriculum in lower-level mathematics classes is about rote learning, worksheets, and procedures. Instruction is designed to control behavior, rather than promote ambitious learning. Advanced mathematics courses on the other hand are oftentimes rich with a problem-based or more conceptually based curriculum; however Black girls are not often found in such courses. And, like it or not, numerous economists and other education researchers have shown that mathematical skills, high school coursework, and college majors predict an individual's labor market earnings.[47] And while BlackFMP is not a neoliberal project, consequences still abound as it relates to Black girls' future economic mobility.

What we know is that Black girls infrequently experience ambitious instruction, instruction focused on "rich representations of content and authentic disciplinary practices, like justifying arguments, representing ideas, and modeling problems in the world."[48] Ambitious mathematics teaching can afford Black girls' genuine opportunities to develop into strong mathematicians. A rigorous mathematics curriculum has the ability to promote higher-order thinking, engage students, reduce discipline problems, and build Black girls' capacity to learn and take intellectual risks; however, it does nothing to dismantle gendered anti-Blackness, promote Black excellence, or celebrate Black girlhood, so ambitious teaching cannot be done in isolation. This is the key reason this dimension is last.

CONCLUSION

The Black girl quotes illuminated that they want to learn in an environment that allows for a more relaxed atmosphere with teachers who hold high expectations that they will learn rigorous mathematics. Black girls desire a teacher who employs ambitious instruction, not direct instruction. Teachers should stop using worksheets for the purposes of regurgitating knowledge, practicing procedures, and memorizing formulas, but this is the reality for many Black girls enrolled in public schools across our nation. This chapter provided one model, BlackFMP, for teachers to use and implement in solidarity with Black girls to improve these outcomes. BlackFMP is not a panacea; working together, its dimensions can support Black girl joy in mathematics. Educators have the capacity to start a radical solidarity project for Black girls in mathematics whereby they flourish in their humanity and brilliance, unfettered by gendered anti-Blackness and white supremacy. I encourage you to join the movement.

5

"YOUR ACT SCORES CAN STOP YOU FROM GOING TO COLLEGE"

Standardized Testing and the Promise of Black Girls' Advancement

The explosion of high-stakes standardized testing in US public education has undermined the ongoing quest to improve the educational outcomes for Black girls. Since their inception a century ago, standardized tests have been instruments of racism and a biased system.[1] Students of color, particularly those from low-income families, have suffered the most from high-stakes testing in US public schools.[2] But the fight of ridding our system of standardized assessment in not my lane; however, it is my fight to illuminate what is problematic about our standardized assessment system and what we might do to better support Black girls within our broken system.

As I am writing this chapter, the US is still in the middle of the COVID-19 global pandemic—a health, economic, political, and educational crisis that disproportionately impacted Black communities. In the spring of 2020, many schools in the US transitioned to online learning, and the underlying disparities from structural and institutionalized racism came front and center. For example, Grace, a fifteen-year-old Black girl from Michigan, was incarcerated for violating her probation—not for fighting, not for stealing, but for failing to complete her online homework.[3] This is just one example of how our system undermines Black girls' educational outcomes. The fact is that Grace will be required to take the Michigan state standardized assessment this year and will likely fail. Although the federal government granted a "blanket waiver" to every state to skip the mandated statewide testing for 2019–2020, the Biden administration recently confirmed that assessment, accountability, and reporting systems would resume for the 2020–2021 academic year.[4]

This chapter sheds light on how the US mathematics assessment system has directly harmed Black girls. The chapter also discusses the ways high-stakes testing and mandated performance requirements often narrow the mathematics curriculum and instruction that teachers enact. High-stakes mathematics testing, then, is part of a larger assessment system that has far-reaching consequences for Black girls, particularly around gifted and talented programs' acceptance, advanced mathematics course enrollment, and college and career plans. As discussed in chapter 3, when mathematics teachers are relegated to use scripts or direct instruction, they can communicate to Black girls that a curriculum focused on deeper thinking through inquiry-based experiences and problem solving (i.e., ambitious instruction) is not for them. And a narrowed mathematics curriculum can significantly reduce Black girls' opportunities to show higher-order thinking skills as well as meet college and career benchmarks on state, federal, and college entrance exams. The chapter closes with how we might push back on the standardized mathematics assessment system by leveraging effective formative assessment strategies and tools as sources of evidence of Black girls' knowledge in mathematics.

PROBLEMATIZING "MATHEMATICS FOR ALL" RHETORIC THROUGH BLACK GIRLS' ACHIEVEMENT

In 2009, the Common Core State Standards for Mathematics (CCSSM) were developed by a team of state-led leaders from across forty-eight states, two territories, and the District of Columbia.[5] By 2021, forty-one states, the District of Colombia, and four territories adopted these standards into practice. The CCSSM presented a record opportunity for systemic improvement in mathematics education in the United States.

This initiative sought to: (a) promote the standardization of conceptual understanding in mathematics, (b) establish a minimum threshold of learning, (c) provide clear and consistent guidelines, and (d) prepare *all* students for college and career after high school graduation.[6] The National Council of Teachers of Mathematics (NCTM) endorsed the CCSSM and invested in several initiatives to ensure that all school districts across the country understood how the CCSSM synergized with NCTM's signature publications, specifically *Principles and Standards for School Mathematics, Curriculum Focal Points, and Focus in High School Mathematics,* published in 2000, 2006, and 2011, respectively.[7] Additionally, in 2010, NCTM convened other national mathematics education organizations, including representatives from NCTM, the National Council of Supervisors of Mathematics (NCSM), the Association of Mathematics Teacher Educators (AMTE), and the Association of State Supervisors of Mathematics (ASSM). This joint task force produced a report that identified priority actions and resources to support teachers, teacher leaders and educators, school and district leaders, and parents.[8]

One of those urgent actions was to convene an *assessment working group* to coordinate the field's best guidance on assessment development and ensure that new student assessments really did address the priorities of the Standards for Mathematical Practice (SMPs) articulated in CCSSM. Remember that the SMPs describe varieties of expertise that mathematics educators at all levels should seek to develop in their students. These practices are important processes and proficiencies relevant to students' development of mathematical ideas, but also for everyday life. The first of these are the NCTM process standards of problem solving, reasoning and proof, communication, representation, and connections. The second are the strands of mathematical proficiency: adaptive reasoning, strategic competence, conceptual understanding (comprehension of mathematical concepts, operations, and relations), procedural fluency (skill in carrying out procedures flexibly, accurately, efficiently, and appropriately), and productive disposition (habitual inclination to see mathematics as sensible, useful, and worthwhile, coupled with a belief in diligence and one's own efficacy).[9]

Part of the assessment working group included a collaboration with the Partnership for Assessment of Readiness for College and Careers

(PARCC) and SMARTER Balanced Assessment State Consortium, the two testing companies that school districts had to choose between when they adopted the CCSSM.[10] In 2010, NCTM's president at the time, J. Michael Shaughnessy, stated:

> NCTM and three other mathematics education organizations worked together on producing this Joint Task Force report. At a time in the history of mathematics education, when it is important to work closely with other organizations, we are positioned to merge our strengths to promote excellence and equity in mathematics teaching and learning for *all* [italics added] students in every school in our nation.[11]

US mathematics education policy organizations have been promoting *equity for all* for twenty years now, yet we know that standardized testing has continued to produce evidence of a subpar mathematics education for most Black girls.[12] Figure 5.1 shows the National Assessment of Education Progress (NAEP) mathematics scores among fourth-grade Black students for the last nine years in the five states with the largest 2018–2019 public school enrollment of Black girls.[13] NAEP is administered every two years and is the largest continuing and nationally representative summative assessment of what US students know and can do in various subjects. It is a congressionally mandated project administered by the National Center for Education Statistics, within the Institute of Education Sciences of the US Department of Education. The first national administration of NAEP occurred in 1969.[14]

Although NAEP and other standardized assessments are important for showing how various racial groups are doing nationally, a critical problem with these data is that the scores are seldom disaggregated at the intersection of race and gender; thus, engaging in a national conversation about Black girls' mathematics assessment patterns and achievement is difficult. Given this fact, these NAEP mathematics scores suggest that many Black girls are not supported to demonstrate proficiency on standardized mathematics tests. These numbers get worse and continue to decline in eighth grade (see figure 5.2). For example, the average score difference between fourth-grade Black students and NAEP mathematics

FIGURE 5.1 Fourth-grade Black students' NAEP scores for District of Columbia, Georgia, Louisiana, Maryland, and Mississippi, 2003–2019

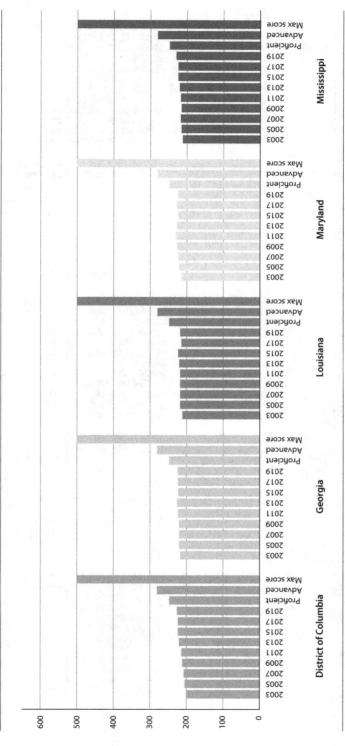

*To be considered Proficient or Advanced by NAEP scoring rubrics, students need a total score of 249 and 282, respectively. The total mathematics score is 500. The 2001 data were not available.

FIGURE 5.2 Eighth-grade Black students' NAEP scores for District of Columbia, Georgia, Louisiana, Maryland, and Mississippi, 2003–2019

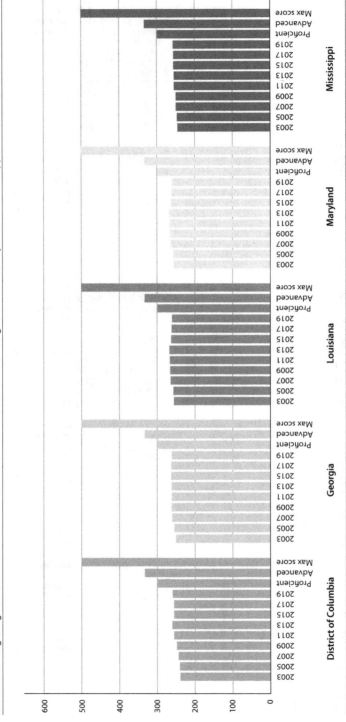

*To be considered Proficient or Advanced by NAEP scoring rubrics, students need a total score of 299 and 333, respectively. The total mathematics score is 500. The 2001 data were not available.

proficiency is about 20 points. The average score difference between Black students and NAEP proficiency grows to about 45 points in the eighth grade. For the 2019 administration year, not one state had average scores for fourth- or eighth-grade Black students that met the mathematics proficiency score of 249 and 299, respectively.

Therefore, the message of *equity for all* has been promised since 2000 but, as of 2021, still has not been realized for most Black girls in US mathematics classrooms, and their underperformance on mathematics assessments continue to happen under NCTM's watch.[15] Every school district should pay attention and work to transform the mathematics education of Black girls in their schools; however, the District of Columbia, Georgia, Louisiana, Maryland, and Mississippi, the five states with the largest enrollment of Black girls, might take more serious action steps to acknowledge the systemic problems and to work to improve Black girls' mathematics learning.

BLACK GIRLS' READINESS FOR COLLEGE: WHAT IS THE STORY?

Preparing all students for college is at the center of mathematics standards reform. College readiness is what higher education institutions consider when making decisions about acceptance. The top four areas that admission committees consider are (a) overall high school grade point average (GPA), (b) grades in college preparatory courses, (c) admission test scores, and (d) strength of the high school curriculum. Factors such as the personal essay, teacher letters of recommendation, extracurricular activities, and students' interests may be talked about as carrying weight, but the truth is they are still secondary considerations.[16] Figure 5.3 shows how these factors vary in importance when colleges make admission decisions.

Black girls' experiences and performances on the primary factors for college readiness reveal significant disparities in mathematics achievement, and these disparities are rooted in racialized and gendered narratives.[17] Research shows that Black students in the United States have the lowest high school GPAs in general and in mathematics, specifically, compared to all groups.[18] The most recent data available from 2016 show that the US median high school GPA is 3.0 and Black students'

FIGURE 5.3   Primary and secondary college-readiness factors

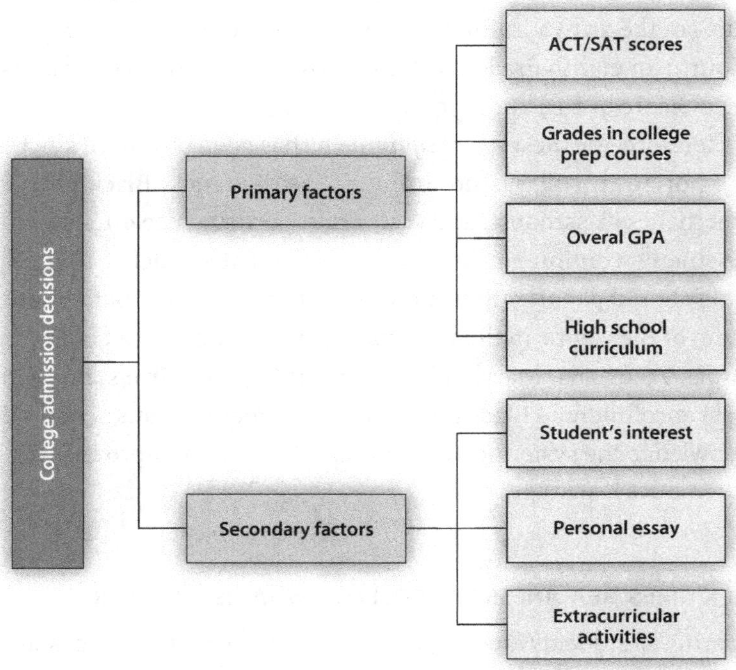

median GPA is 2.69, with a national median high school GPA of 2.65 in mathematics for all students.[19] We also know that most Black girls are not found in college prep courses; thus their ACT test scores suffer. The logic is clear: Black girls need access to advanced mathematics courses that use a high-quality mathematics curriculum, coupled with high-quality mathematics instruction to do well on standardized assessments. As a reminder from chapter 3, a high-quality mathematics curriculum and instruction alone do nothing for Black girls' development of critical conscious thinking to critique the status quo or for honoring their full humanities; they just get Black girls to the basics of a good mathematics education, not a transformative mathematics education.

Narratives that prioritize a narrow view of Black girls' college readiness originate from mathematics achievement scores backed by research, and those narratives often miss the complex understandings of Black girls' intersectional experiences. Although there have been some shifts to include contextualization in mathematics education research focused on Black girls, TV journalists and social media report on test scores and interpret annual findings, resting on meritocratic thinking and overgeneralizations of their meanings. Much as in the notion of the American Dream, those who ascribe to the notion of meritocracy assume success is primarily determined by hard work, while ignoring hidden unearned advantages and inequitable structures that lead to disparate outcomes.[20] *Meritocracy* assumes a level playing field by suggesting that one's work ethic, values, drive, and individual attributes (such as aptitude and intelligence scores) determine success or failure.[21] All too often, this meritocratic mind-set frames the thinking and decision-making of K–12 educators and leaders who regard these testing and achievement gaps based on perception of work ethic or ability, rather than by design.[22] Because meritocratic lines of thought are divorced from critical mathematics education research that calls into question the decontextualized stories about mathematics achievement, such stories are dangerous. The danger of only pointing out racial disparities without considering the conditions that created the outcomes in the first place continues academic harm for Black girls.

BLACK GIRLS AND ASSESSMENT SOCIALIZATION: A CASE EXAMPLE OF THE ACT

Interpreting Black girls' mathematics test scores, specifically, is a complex process my colleague and I have termed *assessment socialization*.[23] What we mean by assessment socialization is the lifelong process of inheriting and disseminating norms, customs, and ideologies associated with schooling practices and institutional structures.[24] For example, all Black girls enrolled in public schools across the United States engage in being socialized to the norms of assessments, and as such, they develop some sense of their purpose over time. Mathematics students complete assessments at the end of chapters and units, they complete statewide summative assessments, and, in most districts, most students are required to complete a benchmark assessment at the completion of a quarter or semester. Thus,

Black girls are socialized to engage in assessment activities because they are a part of the structures of schools and assessments that are supposed to reveal what students know and can do.

It is well documented in the literature that summative assessments indicate a vastly too narrow definition of knowledge that influences course-taking trajectories, leading many students, and disproportionally Black girls, into tracked lower-level mathematics courses.[25] The teaching and learning experiences for students in the lower-level courses vary greatly in terms of rigor, expectations, content, and beliefs.[26] As a result of experiences in disproportionate tracking, courses with lack of rigor, content, and beliefs in students' abilities, many Black girls come to be shaped or socialized by a discourse associated with the system (i.e., low-level courses are for stupid kids), thereby potentially enacting a self-fulfilling prophecy.[27] Counselors and teachers alike often do not take responsibility for supporting Black girls and their families in understanding the long-term consequences when they are enrolled in lower-level courses.[28] An important example of those consequences is ineligibility to apply to certain selective higher education institutions. But other and more significant consequences might be that Black girls do not receive a high-quality mathematics education, which can eclipse future opportunities for STEM college majors and/or high-paying job opportunities that require important mathematics literacy skills.

The following excerpts are from a focus group of Black girls discussing their experiences and talking about what kinds of things get in the way of accomplishing their future college and career goals. These data come from a recent study conducted with forty-eight high school Black girls that aimed to learn about their mathematics experiences in urban schools.[29] The ACT is a central theme of these data; thus the rationale for highlighting it as an example of a standardized assessment for college and career readiness. The ACT assesses four content areas: English, mathematics, reading, and science, with an optional writing section. These tests are designed to measure skills that are most important for success in postsecondary education. The score range for each of the four multiple-choice tests is 1–36. The overall or composite score is the average of the four test scores rounded to the nearest whole number. Although the girls are not specifically speaking about mathematics per se, what they have learned in mathematics and how that learning translates to a score on the mathematics section of the ACT will matter significantly. The following conversation is among Black girls in the focus group:

Black Girl: "It could be—some people, it's like their grades and their GPAs and stuff. It could be like your ACT scores that can stop you from going to a certain college."

Black Girl: "That is so rigged. I don't like ACT."

Black Girl: "I feel like people are actually really smart, but *their grades don't reflect their intelligence* [emphasis added]. And I feel like it's—the system is rigged."

Black Girl: "Or they can be really smart, and they just don't have a strive to do anything or they're not motivated, so they can actually [inaudible]."

Black Girl: "I feel like at the school it's a lot of smart people, but then the *classes we take, they just don't reflect on actually how smart we are* emphasis added], so then our grades—like [inaudible] somebody that could go to East and they're making As and Bs."

Black Girl: "Oh, man. Then they come here."

Black Girl: "And they struggle."

Black Girl: "And then they come here, and then like they don't make As and Bs no more."

Black Girl: "Like where them As go?"

Black Girl: "They're going Ds to Fs."

Black Girl: "And Cs."

Black Girl: "I feel like it's just here or [inaudible]. They put too much stress on this."

This particular focus group included Black girls enrolled in advanced mathematics courses in their schools. Research shows how gifted and talented programs can help Black girls reach their potential, specifically with academic achievement, socialization, and future success, yet this conversation the Black girls are having reveals something different—that their smartness or gifts go unnoticed.[30] Their dialogue demonstrates that their full potential is yet to be realized. Their responses pointed directly to systems and structures embedded in white supremacy culture (chapter 2)—individualism and objectivity—through individual grades and standardized assessment scores in this case. As emphasized in chapter 1, the US mathematics education system dehumanizes Black girls in multiple ways and makes them invisible, promoting marginalization and detriment. Overall, these quotes reveal that Black girls understand that the education systems they are a part of does not love them and does not provide opportunities for them to demonstrate their genius.

The next conversation is from a different focus group of high school Black girls, who were also placed in advanced mathematics courses. In responding to the question, "How are you learning about what you might do after high school?" they shared that they were responsible for figuring out most of the information on their own. Again, the ACT is important in their conversation.

> **Black Girl:** "We have to teach ourself."
>
> **Black Girl:** "They don't even know their own statistics, like how to get you into a college and what you need as long as you show up and—or how they want you to look and go to class, and that's it. They think they did their job. But . . ."
>
> **Black Girl:** "Yeah."
>
> **Black Girl:** "We have to ask like an administrator that's not over the discipline area. We have to ask a counselor or somebody. And that takes time out of our day to go and ask what we have to do to get where we want to be. And it's very few teachers that would take the time out just to help students with their life outside of school or with college or with doing ACT or SAT, whatever. But the teachers themselves . . ."
>
> **Black Girl:** "Are selfish."
>
> **Black Girl:** "We see every other day or on a daily basis, they don't try to help [us] at all."
>
> **Black Girl:** "And it's like we take the—most of us take the ACT this year and though I think most of the junior class is ready, not really. And even if you try to go talk to someone, mostly they just tell us oh, guys, we have an ACT book, like that was what the principal said directly.

We had this huge assembly, and she was like we take the ACT, da, da, da, da, da. You should purchase an ACT book. A student purchased it. They scored this because they read from a book. *It's like it's not really them teaching you. It's you teaching yourself* [emphasis added]."

Black Girl: "Yeah, I'm in ACT prep class, the class you actually came and got me out of. One, we're in a class that we don't have a teacher that'll help us to strategize or teach us how to do the ACT prep or what strategies to use. We just have a sub in there and we don't do nothing in there, so what's the point of the class if you're not going to learn?"

Black Girl: "The subs here, they're just really here to supervise."

Moderator: *"OK. So they just—"*

Black Girl: "Supervise."

Black Girl: "They're here for the school not to be shut down."

Black Girl: "To make sure we don't do nothing."

Black Girl: "Yeah. They took us out of the class that had a teacher, and he really didn't do nothing. He gave us a word for the day, told us to write it down. Three synonyms, three sentences, that was about it. He didn't try to take the time out to break the strategies down. He didn't take time to teach the strategies or nothing. He just wanted us to practice doing the actual test, and that was it, and doing a word. That was it."

Black Girl: "Yeah, he gave us an ACT book and he was like this is how much time you got on this, so do it."

Black Girl: "And when the time ends, you'll stop."

This dialogue between the girls and the interviewer reveals the ways that schools continue to fail Black girls. In the next section, I discuss the connections between standards, content, instruction, and assessment and why the experiences the girls shared are consequential to college and career goals. The girls were responsible for teaching themselves, and the adults in their schools did not ensure a productive ACT prep experience. While an ACT prep class is only one aspect of the preparation for college and career, it is a critical part, and they know that. Their experiences help to shed light on their understanding of the ACT as an important factor that can get in the way of their future aspirations. Their perspectives clearly communicate that if their opportunities to learn are minimized and diminished, the point of school diminishes.

Black girls need teachers and administrators who understand the social-political context of Black girlhood and the systematic ways their humanities are degraded in schools. This is how what might appear as normative practices of schooling—ineffective counselors and substitutes—creates a unique experience for Black girls. Additionally, action is needed to address the atrocities many Black girls face in trying to figure out what they need to do to be prepared for college and careers. Much work needs to be done to improve Black girls' mathematics education and standardized assessment experiences.

THE DISCONNECT BETWEEN STANDARDS, CURRICULUM, INSTRUCTION, AND ASSESSMENT

The previous section showed that the US mathematics education system is failing Black girls, socializing them into an assessment system that does not benefit or prioritize their college and career readiness. Educators either are not equipped or refuse to support Black girls in understanding the inextricable links between mathematics content, instruction, and assessments. While on the one hand, the ACT is regarded as a curriculum-based test (usually aligned to subject-area national standards) that can assess students' mastery of both college and career readiness standards, on the other hand, the ACT remains *norm-referenced*, meaning that the mathematics score, for example, compares how a Black girl performs against everyone else who takes the exam in any particular year.[31] Norm-referenced tests are specifically designed to rank test-takers on a bell curve, or a distribution of scores that resembles the outline of a bell when graphed—that is, a small percentage of students performing well, most performing average, and a small percentage performing poorly. To produce a bell curve each time, ACT test questions are carefully designed to accentuate performance differences among test-takers, not to determine whether students have achieved specified learning standards, learned certain material, or acquired specific skills and knowledge.[32]

A Black girl may not understand these complexities of the ACT and how connections between what mathematics curriculum she is taught, how that curriculum is taught, and how instructional experiences shape her ACT performance on the mathematics section. If a Black girl took the ACT in 2020 and received an overall score of 30, then she had a ninety-third percentile ranking, which means she performed the same as or higher than 93 percent of the other students who took the test that year (a very high score). Additionally, a score of 30 would have placed her in the eighty-ninth percentile in English, a ninety-fourth percentile in mathematics, an eighty-sixth percentile in reading, and a ninety-third percentile in science for the 2020 administration.

A closer look at mathematics is important. Table 5.1 is a replication of the number and quantity standards table on the ACT website that describes what students who score in specific ranges on the mathematics section of the ACT college-readiness assessment are likely to know and be able to do as it pertains to skills and knowledge.[33] It should be noted that other strands include algebra and functions, geometry, and probability and statistics.

Black girls need access to advanced mathematics to increase their scores. Table 5.1 demonstrates that higher mathematics ACT scores are evidence of access to rigorous curriculum and high-quality mathematics learning experiences—neither of which Black girls experience often enough. To make the college-readiness benchmark of 22 on the mathematics portion of the ACT, Black girls should know all the standards listed in the first three rows of table 5.1. How can they master those standards if they are not given adequate access to the content? Students who earn 22 on the mathematics portion are more likely to earn an overall ACT average that is above 22. Nationally, while most community colleges do not require the ACT, if Black girls are interested in community colleges' more selective programs, such as nursing or the sciences, the ACT is likely required.[34] Additionally, if Black girls plan to transfer to a four-year institution, the ACT is likely required.[35] Black girls scoring above 22 open other opportunities for scholarships. College funders identify hundreds of public scholarships available to students with composite ACT scores of 22 or higher.[36]

TABLE 5.1 The American College Testing (ACT) Readiness Standards for Mathematics—Number and quantity strand and possible scores

ACT SCORE	TOPICS IN THE FLOW TO NUMBER AND QUANTITY (N)	INTERPRETATION
13–15	• N201. Perform one-operation computation with whole numbers and decimals • N 202. Recognize equivalent fractions and fractions in lowest terms • N203. Locate positive rational numbers (expressed as whole numbers, fractions, decimals, and mixed numbers) on the number line	Students who score in the 1–12 range are most likely beginning to develop the knowledge and skills assessed in the other ranges.
16–19	• N301. Recognize one-digit factors of a number • N302. Identify a digit's place value • N303. Locate rational numbers on the number line • Note: A matrix as a representation of data is treated here as a basic table	
20–23	• N401. Exhibit knowledge of elementary number concepts such as rounding, the ordering of decimals, pattern identification, primes, and greatest common factor • N402. Write positive powers of 10 by using exponents • N403. Comprehend the concept of length on the number line, and find the distance between two points • N404. Understand absolute value in terms of distance • N405. Find the distance in the coordinate plane between two points with the same x-coordinate or y-coordinate • N406. Add two matrices that have whole number entries	The ACT College Readiness Benchmark for Mathematics is 22. Students who achieve at least a 22 on the ACT Mathematics Test have a 50% likelihood of achieving a B or better in a first-year College Algebra course at a typical college.
24–27	• N501. Order fractions • N502. Find and use the least common multiple • N503. Work with numerical factors • N504. Exhibit some knowledge of the complex numbers • N505. Add and subtract matrices that have integer entries	
28–32	• N601. Apply number properties involving prime factorization • N602. Apply number properties involving even/odd numbers and factors/multiples • N603. Apply number properties involving positive/negative numbers • N604. Apply the facts that π is irrational and that the square root of an integer is rational only if that integer is a perfect square • N605. Apply properties of rational exponents • N606. Multiply two complex numbers • N607. Use relations involving addition, subtraction, and scalar multiplication of vectors and of matrices	Students who achieve the 28–32 level are likely able to use variables fluently so that they can solve problems with variables in the same way that they can solve the problems with numbers, and they can use variables to represent general properties.

TABLE 5.1 *Continued*

ACT SCORE	TOPICS IN THE FLOW TO NUMBER AND QUANTITY (N)	INTERPRETATION
33–36	• N701. Analyze and draw conclusions based on number concepts • N702. Apply properties of rational numbers and the rational number system • N703. Apply properties of real numbers and the real number system, including properties of irrational numbers • N704. Apply properties of complex numbers and the complex number system • N705. Multiply matrices • N706. Apply properties of matrices and properties of matrices as a number system	

Source: For more information about the ACT College and Career Readiness Standards in Mathematics, go to www.act.org/standard/planact/math/mathnotes.html.

Because many Black girls are forced to learn about college readiness on their own, they miss important conversations about curricular exposure—mathematics in this case—and what mathematics content is needed to score at or above a 22 on the ACT. ACT (and SAT) are summative standardized tests that attempt to measure what students know overall. But the ACT and SAT do nothing to inform teachers' daily instruction, nor have they been shown to support Black girls' understanding about what they know and can do in mathematics, not to mention what areas are needed to improve test scores. In contrast to summative standardized tests, formative assessments examine learning along the way and can be powerful ways for Black girls to become independent and metacognitive thinkers, problem solvers, and assessors of their own mathematics knowledge. The next section discusses the affordances of formative assessments for illuminating Black girls' mathematical knowledge.

THE STRENGTHS OF FORMATIVE ASSESSMENTS FOR "SEEING" BLACK GIRLS' MATHEMATICS DEVELOPMENT

Standardized testing, such as the ACT and SAT, will likely never go away. What can mathematics teachers, general educators, Black girls and their families, and other constituents committed to Black girl liberation do to support increasing their future assessment scores? One answer is to use formative assessments early when Black girls are preschoolers and to continue to expose and develop their mathematics knowledge over time using various assessments for learning. There have been several meta-analyses conducted on formative assessment literature; however, the 1998 study by Paul Black and Dylan Wiliam is most cited (11,292 times as of April 2021) as evidence for the positive impact formative assessment practices can have on student achievement.[37] These scholars found that high-quality formative assessments improved scores on standardized tests between 0.4 and 0.7 percent, a greater impact than most known educational interventions.[38] Although there are different definitions, methodological issues, and disagreements in the formative assessment literature, what matters is that formative assessments do offer some level of efficacy for increasing students' mathematics achievement.[39]

"Formative assessment" can be traced back to the late 1960s when Benjamin Bloom argued that 90 percent of students can master what teachers teach and that *instruction* can find the means which will enable students to master the subject under consideration.[40] Almost fifty years later in 2007, the late griot Dr. Asia G. Hilliard III pushed Bloom's statement further to point out that "our [Black] children, if respected, and if exposed to good teaching, have the genius to master any content, even alien content."[41] Formative assessments are a part of good teaching and instruction; thus, they are critical for mastery and deep learning of mathematics concepts and skills. Formative assessments include formal and informal, graded and nongraded evaluations, tasks, and quizzes used by teachers to gather information about individual student needs, progress, and comprehension. Formative assessments are used to inform teachers what they might do next in their instruction, both for whole-group and for individual learning. Self-assessments are a type of formative assessment whereby students articulate what they know and what they are still learning. Thus, I position formative assessments as one of the most effective strategies that teachers, Black girls, and their families can use to support Black girls' enhanced development of mathematical ideas, skills, and concepts. Using different types of formative assessments could not only develop Black girls' mathematical knowledge, but also normalize mathematics learning, especially NCTM's process standards: problem solving, communication, reasoning, representation, and connections.[42]

The key difference between summative and formative assessments is the timing of *student feedback* and decision-making about outcomes. For example, the results of state or college admission tests are not known for months. End-of-course summative exams are often used only to determine a final grade in a course, without thought of concepts mastered or lessons learned. These summative assessments give a snapshot of one moment in time. Summative assessments are also high stakes because major decisions affecting a student's life are made, decisions such as high school graduation, grade promotion, gifted or talented programs, and college admissions. In contrast, formative assessments can be nonevaluative, specific, timely, and goal related so that students have opportunities to revise and improve their work and deepen their understanding.[43] But, unfortunately, the literature suggests that teachers often do not understand how to use formative assessments in a structured way in their daily teaching practice to support student learning.[44] Consequently, teachers need to gain an understanding of formative assessments and implement them to help Black girls grow into strong mathematics learners through productive use of feedback.

Some categories of formative assessments include oral conversations, entry-exit tickets, Pear Deck slides, classwork tasks, and group-work tasks. Families already use formative assessments with their children. For example, when parents ask their three- and four-year-old children to "count the stop lights" or "count the trees" as they drive home, the parents are engaging in a simple, but integrated type of formative assessment. The parent aims to understand if and how far their child can count; the assessment is integrated because counting and driving home in the car is a natural and regular family activity. Parents also often provide immediate feedback through praise or questions. For teachers, formative assessment data can also be gathered through a student's thumb-up, -down, or -sideways response to a mathematics question. Formative assessments can be quite simple, super elaborate, or somewhere in the middle. There are hundreds of ways to formatively assess students' learning, but teachers should make sure that they are aligned with state or national standards. Table 5.2 provides a few examples of different formative assessments. I identify a learning standard, materials, and possible student feedback. Note that these activities could be used to introduce a new mathematics idea and/or used to practice with reflective components, such as oral conversations or mathematics journals. Table 5.3 organizes and categorizes different strategies for types of evidence.

Feedback from formative assessments can be used to support Black girls' mathematics achievement. For example, using the think-pair-share

TABLE 5.2   Examples of formative assessments for mathematics learning

FORMATIVE ASSESSMENTS	SAMPLE CCSSM AND SAMPLE GRADE LEVEL	MATERIALS	SAMPLE FEEDBACK
Exploring notices and wonders	• Know groupings within 10 • Counting • K–12th grade	• Deck of cards	Ask: What do you know about making groups of 10? What do you notice while counting? What do you wonder about?
Think-pair-share	• Analyze proportional relationships and use them to solve real-world and mathematical problems • 7th–10th grade	• Outside space, paper, and pencil, partner groups	Ask: How many jumping jacks can you do in 60 seconds? Now, pair up with a peer and share your numbers. What is your rate of jumping jacks? Pairs discuss findings with the whole class.
Which one doesn't belong?	• Analyze characteristics of content being studied • K–12th grade	• A square broken into four equal sections with different numbers, graphs, pictures, etc., that show a relationship among three of the items	State: Find a reason why one doesn't belong with the other three. Justify your decisions with pictures, words, and/or numbers.
Always sometimes never	• Analyze statements related to various math ideas • 3rd–12th grade	• From one to however many the teacher decides, math statements for the students to analyze	Ask: Is this statement always true, sometimes, true, or never true? Justify your conclusions with examples or counterexamples.

TABLE 5.3 Formative assessments by type

TYPE OF EVIDENCE	NAME OF STRATEGY
Student Work	*Three things* • List 3 things that a peer might misunderstand about the topic.
	Venn diagram • Have students compare or contrast a topic using a Venn diagram.
	Expansion projects • Extension projects such as a poster or collage to provide additional ways to demonstrate understanding of a concept.
	Metacognition • Metacognition allows for students to process what they did in class and why it was done. At the end of the assignment, have students complete and provide feedback on a table that the teacher can collect. What did we do? Why did we do it? What did I learn? How can I apply it? What questions do I still have about it?
	Entry/exit tickets • Exit tickets have one or more questions at the end of the lesson for students to complete and teacher collects.
Technology	*Poll Everywhere* • Use Poll Everywhere or Google Docs to ask questions during class and have students respond individually (or in groups) to the questions.
	Pear Deck/Near Pod • Use Pear Deck or Near Pod to have students reply to questions during class in an interactive format. While this is like Poll Everywhere, each interface is different.
	Text the answer • Students text their answer to an interactive message board, such as Wiffiti—the Interactive Message Board—Classroom 2.0 (classroom20.com). It hides their identity so that students can be honest and not feel embarrassed.
Peers	*Teach other kids* • Have students teach other students, sometimes younger (or act as tutors), to explore how they would explain their thinking. Check with both sets of students to see how well it worked. Use this to inform your instruction for the older or younger students.
	Rotate groups • Have students work in stations and rotate through the stations. In small groups, facilitate a discussion and assess students in small groups. Additionally, provide everyone in the group with feedback.

(continues)

TABLE 5.3 *Continued*

TYPE OF EVIDENCE	NAME OF STRATEGY
Teacher Observations	*Ask clarifying questions* • Ask questions of students to clarify your understanding of student thinking. Record these in a way that will allow you to return to inform instruction. *Shuffle quiz* • Ask students to study or work on a task together. When the teacher comes over, they can shuffle student papers and randomly select one student to share out their mathematical thinking. If the teacher would like the group to keep working, they ask them to do so and then return.
Teacher Feedback	*Comments* Write descriptive comments on student work, including individual and group tasks, and quizzes, helping them see how they can improve their work or what they have done that really worked for them.

to activate prior knowledge means that the facilitator or teachers can see what the girls already know about rates and ratios. Girls sharing and fielding questions is another place for teachers to take notes about their understanding of the specified learning standards. The teacher can list individual students and/or pairs to follow up with in the next math class to share feedback. Note, these processes need to be taught to the girls and practiced over and over until they become routine. Figuring out the best process to structure and facilitate giving and receiving meaningful feedback is significant because not all feedback is equal. Feedback should provide Black girls opportunities to critically reflect on their mathematics learning and ask follow-up questions. While learning new mathematics topics, Black girls should have an opportunity to recall, ponder, and communicate about these and their own mathematical ideas. Sentence stems, such as "I like how you did X because . . . " or "I wonder how X relates to Y" could be used to scaffold some ways of what it means to reflect on mathematical ideas. Such experiences can position Black girls as co-constructors of mathematical knowledge. Using formative assessments develops strong mathematical thinking and process skills in Black girls, which can increase the likelihood of them earning mathematics ACT scores at 22 or higher.

CONCLUSION

Standardized mathematics assessments have historically eclipsed and sabotaged Black girls' genius. Over time, traditional forms of assessment have harmed Black girls, in part because their scores are often at the lowest level of the mathematics achievement hierarchy. The resulting narratives that get constructed through public media, including schools' websites and local news stories, have characterized Black girls as deficient or inferior. Correcting this narrative requires us to take to task the mathematics organizations and national leadership who talk about "equity for all," but have yet to make changes that will make this a reality for Black girls. The examination of Black girls' assessment socialization experiences in mathematics contexts reveals how ideologies and structures get in the way of them having access to advanced mathematics content and powerful mathematics instructors.

A growing number of colleges and universities, such as Harvard and Cornell, are waiving SAT and ACT requirements for 2021 applicants due to COVID-19.[45] The University of California system phased out SAT and ACT admissions requirements through 2024.[46] This pause is an excellent opportunity for educators to consider whether these types of assessments are necessary or if they are simply harmful overall. The hiatus is likely to be short-lived if given colleges' reverence for national rankings and the volume of applications selective universities receive; therefore, standardized assessments are not likely to be completely dismantled in our educational system.

Given this reality, this chapter also sought to leverage formative assessments as one significant tool to use with Black girls while learning mathematics. Providing Black girls feedback that helps them answer essential questions, *Where am I going? How am I going?* And *Where to next?* is critical when there is a discrepancy between what they understand and where they need to be in accomplishing mathematics learning objectives and standards.[47] The type of assessment feedback that is needed attends to metacognition and self-regulation, offering the potential for Black girls to further engage with or invest further effort into the mathematics learning enterprise. Proper assessment support can also enhance Black girls' self-efficacy and attributions that the feedback is deserved and earned.

When feedback draws attention to the monitoring processes needed to engage with a mathematical task, Black girls' beliefs about the importance of effort and their conceptions of mathematics learning can be important arbiters in the learning process and, ultimately, achievement. These are the types of experiences Black girls need to self-actualize into strong mathematical learners.

6

A TALK TO MATHEMATICS TEACHERS WHO ARE READY TO GO FOR BROKE

A student will perform for a teacher who they think respects them, someone with whom they can relate, and someone with whom they feel a connection. Sometimes that connection is because of the subject, because of the ethnicity or gender of the teacher, or because of the teacher's personality. Whatever it is, teachers need to realize that making a connection with Black girls speaks volumes.

—YOLANDA A. JOHNSON[1]

How can teachers show respect, build relationships, and make connections with Black girls when research has shown that sometimes they hold the greatest biases against Black girls when assessing their mathematical ability?[2] In a 2020 study that explored whether teachers' evaluations of their students' mathematical ability or performance were accurate or whether their evaluations revealed implicit biases, Yasemin Copur-Gencturk and colleagues used a randomized controlled study (N = 390) to examine and separate these factors.[3] They explored teachers' evaluations of eighteen mathematical solutions to which gender- and race-specific names had been randomly assigned. Their study concluded that when assessing students' mathematical ability, biases against Black, Hispanic, and white female students were revealed, with biases greatest against girls with Black- and Hispanic-sounding names.[4] These scholars also found that nonwhite teachers' estimations of students' mathematical ability favored white students (both boys and girls) over students of color, whereas primarily white female teachers' estimations of students' mathematical ability favored boys over girls.[5] This study exemplifies how Black girls can suffer from intersectional oppression in mathematics contexts.

American society continues to perpetuate the notion that Black people and girls, specifically, are incapable of doing and being successful in mathematics. Thus, many Black girls experience a unique discrimination in their mathematics experiences. This intersectional oppression is the outcome of several factors including implicit biases and low expectations among teachers, teachers' internalization of societal stereotypes about Black girls, nonexistent positive teacher-student relationships, and other meaningful aspects of Black girls' learning experiences.[6] What happens in K–12 schooling for many Black girls is that they do not receive rigorous instruction and affirming learning environments, which stifles their mathematics learning development and sets them up for placement at the bottom of the mathematics achievement hierarchy.[7]

Sadly, Copur-Gencturk and colleagues' study also revealed that negative views about Black students are not exclusively held by white teachers, but that even teachers of color can internalize deficit perspectives of Black students' mathematics achievement. This happens because everyone's life in the United States is shaped by whiteness and white supremacy (see chapter 2), and because of this, many people of color struggle to engage in critical analyses of the causes of their own oppression.[8] Therefore, many teachers of color also perpetuate the inequalities found in US mathematics classrooms and education systems broadly.[9] That means the work of unlearning and dismantling oppression is the work of all educators regardless of race. *Making Black Girls Count in Math Education* highlights these issues to begin a national and intentional dialogue about how we can go about engaging this work to better support Black girls in our classrooms and schools.

This chapter is a talk to teachers who teach Black girls—preservice and in-service teachers. The chapter is an extension of chapter 4, which explored types of pedagogies Black girls reported valuing for increasing their participation, understanding of mathematical concepts or ideas, and overall development in mathematics. I presented my BlackFMP model in that chapter as one way of responding to Black girls' voices, advancing more creative pedagogies that can move Black girls toward a more liberatory mathematics education. But, using liberatory pedagogies, particularly in mathematics classrooms, requires much ongoing and *critical self-work* on the part of the instructor. The late James Baldwin, who wrote and delivered a speech on October 16, 1963, to New York City teachers called "A Talk to Teachers" inspired this chapter, because his speech provided insights about what critical self-work can look like.[10] He stated:

> The society in which we live is desperately menaced, not by Khrushchev, but from within. To any citizen of this country who figures himself as responsible—and particularly those of you who deal with the minds and hearts of young people—must be prepared to "go for broke."[11]

This conversation is for mathematics teachers of Black girls who (1) acknowledge the role systemic psychosocial, symbolic, intellectual, and psychological violence has played in impeding Black girls' strong mathematics identities and transformative mathematics learning experiences; and (2) want to take action to dismantle the violence—go for broke.[12] Going for broke means that teachers of mathematics directly, explicitly, and creatively through insubordination, call out, confront, and change any adverse impacts on Black girls that burden them psychologically, mentally, culturally, spiritually, economically, or physically. This includes addressing practices, policies, and procedures that prevent Black girls from learning and thus harming them.[13] Sometimes adverse impacts take the form of conventional practices and policies that foster a climate of violence, or policies and practices that appear neutral, but result in discriminatory effects.[14] Going for broke also means that *when*, not if, teachers are met with "the most fantastic, the most brutal, and the most determined resistance," they will never give up.[15] Teachers will not make excuses. Teachers will not blame Black girls and their families. Rather, they will remain vigilant about deconstructing and decentering the structural systems of whiteness and anti-Blackness in mathematics education, not just within the curriculum, but also in the oppressive structures that occur on the macro levels (i.e., tracking of Black girls into lower-level mathematics courses), meso levels (i.e., not recommending Black girls for gifted or talented programs), and micro levels (saying Black girls need more motivation to do better in mathematics, rather than reflecting on teaching practices).

While teachers are decentering whiteness, they are simultaneously working in solidarity with Black girls and their families to provide Black girls with tools to empower themselves into self-actualized young people and adults. While there is a need for all mathematics teachers to consider the intersection of race, gender, and math classrooms, this chapter serves as a starting point for those who are ready to do the work. Teachers who still need to be convinced that the work is even necessary will probably only be brought onboard through broad educational policy change geared toward breaking down systems rooted in white supremacy.

White teachers should be especially careful when engaging in this work, because if their efforts do not include daily interrogations of these systems, coupled with critical reflection and being in community with other like-minded individuals or groups, their endeavors could do more harm than good. Irene Yoon warns teachers, particularly white teachers who have good intentions yet still find themselves displaying contradictions between their intentions and actual words and behaviors.[16] Yoon called this paradox "whiteness-at-work," a term she created to describe the discursive processes observed in a group of white teachers at an elementary school who participated in an all-staff book group aiming to raise awareness and develop cultural competence among school staff.[17] Yoon concluded:

> Whiteness-at-work functioned as a constraining influence even in the midst of conversations about cultural competence. Thus, whiteness-at-work maintained silences in conversations that were ironically intended to discuss race talk. Yet race was a constant player in the room, shaping assumptions and ways of interacting.[18]

Whiteness-at-work is a power structure that must be disrupted and dismantled, but many teachers may not know how to engage in this work in a deep and meaningful way. *Making Black Girls Count in Math*

Education challenges teachers to recognize and dig deep within to create a transformative plan of action that includes developing goals around three components: (a) teacher racial identities, (b) Black girlhood, and (c) rigorous mathematics instruction. Such a plan of action can provide mathematics teachers a landscape of the critical self-work necessary to develop into powerful mathematics teachers for Black girls. In other words, implementing my BlackFMP model or other liberatory pedagogies in mathematics with Black girls first requires that mathematics teachers interrogate the self, histories, systems, interactions, and teaching practices. This work is metacognitive, emotional, intellectual, and even physiological, so the work should not be done in silos, but in community. Working in meaningful learning communities provides spaces to set clear goals, assess those goals, critically reflect, celebrate wins, and then set new goals. Teachers can also receive ongoing feedback as they work toward their goals of becoming outstanding teachers of mathematics of Black girls.

The chapter begins by providing national data on average teacher characteristics in US public schools, including data from the District of Columbia, Georgia, Louisiana, Maryland, and Mississippi, the states with the largest public school enrollment of Black girls (see chapter 4). I also present data on the percentage distribution of teachers by race and the student composition at their schools. I then put all these statistics in conversations with discourses, initiatives, and policies focused on increasing the number of racially diverse teachers generally, mathematics teachers specifically, to illuminate blind spots and gaps in these efforts that often do not consider nuances of recruitment and retention factors of teachers of color of mathematics and Black teachers of mathematics, precisely. Lessons learned from these policy initiatives point to the need for a focus on the three components of the transformative action plan I discussed earlier. I conclude the chapter by detailing these three features of the action plan.

WHO TEACHES IN US SCHOOLS?

The National Teacher and Principal Survey (NTPS) is a nationally representative sample survey of public and private K–12 schools, principals, and teachers in the fifty states and the District of Columbia.[19] NTPS collects data on core topics including teacher and principal preparation, classes taught, school characteristics, and demographics of the teacher and principal labor forces. The National Center for Education Statistics (NCES) of the Institute of Education Sciences (IES) developed the survey; the US Census Bureau conducted it. The purpose of the NTPS is to collect information that can provide a detailed picture of US elementary and secondary schools and their staff. This information is collected through school, principal, and teacher surveys.

The most recent data in the NTPS are from the 2017–2018 administration, and the results showed that the teaching force in the United States is still largely white and female. The average teacher in the US is a forty-three-year-old white woman with about fourteen years of experience.[20] Roughly 79 percent of all public school teachers are white, 7 percent are Black, and 9 percent are Hispanic.[21] Georgia's teachers were 70 percent white, 24.7 percent Black, 2.8 percent Hispanic, and 1 percent Asian.[22] Roughly 72 percent of Louisiana's teachers were white, with 19.9, 2.9, and 1.8 percent Black, Hispanic, and Asian, respectively.[23] Mississippi teachers were 77.2 percent white, 19.9 percent Black, 1.6 percent Hispanic; no data were available for Asian teachers.[24] The District of Columbia and Maryland had survey responses of less than 50 percent, so no data were available.[25] These data suggest that the South has the largest percentages of Black public school teachers, which is not surprising given the origins and history of Black people and migration patterns.[26] Where there are Black communities, you will find Black teachers and educators.[27]

The US teacher demographics stand in stark contrast to student demographics in public schools, as the student population continues to increase racially and ethnically. Figure 6.1 shows what the student and teacher percentage population distribution looked like in 2007 and how it changed a decade later in 2017.[28]

Black student and teacher populations declined from 2007 to 2017. The number of Hispanic students and teachers increased, but overall, the ratio of same-race students to teachers remained disproportional among Black students and teachers. Figure 6.1 shows that while white student and teacher populations also decreased, agreement between the race of

FIGURE 6.1 Percentage comparison of Black, Hispanic, Asian, and white student and teacher populations for school years 2007 and 2017

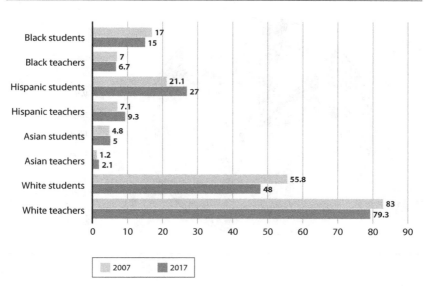

teachers and the majority race of the student population of schools was most pronounced for white teachers during both time frames. Further, the data show that Black teachers continue to not be representative of the nation's Black students enrolled in public schools. In raw numbers, there were 239,000 Black teachers of 3,535,000 total teachers in the 2017–2018 school year (approximately 6.7 percent of all teachers).[29] The number of Black teachers would need to more than double—from 239,000 to roughly 530,000—if their share of the teaching force were to match that of Black students relative to the public school population (3,535,000 x .15). This means that Black girls are more often taught by white teachers, because even at schools with more than 50 percent Black student population, 54 percent of the teachers were white and 36 percent were Black.[30]

The number of Black high school mathematics teachers is bleaker. Figure 6.2 shows the distribution of high school mathematics teachers by race and ethnicity in the United States for 2018.[31] Black mathematics teachers represented only 8 percent in 2018. Two years earlier, in 2016,

FIGURE 6.2 High school mathematics teachers by race and ethnicity in the United States, 2018

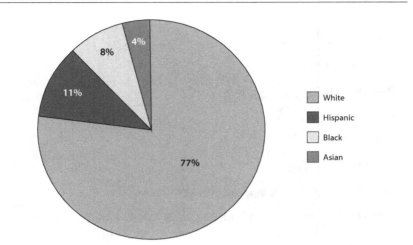

Bisola Neil's dissertation used the 2011–2012 Schools and Staffing Survey (the former name of the NTPS) to identify factors associated with the intent of Black mathematics teachers to turn over.[32] Among other important findings (which I discuss later in this section), Neil found an overwhelming nineteen states *without a single Black mathematics teacher* during the 2011–2012 academic school year.[33] Overall, what these data show is that the majority of mathematics teachers in the United States are white, which has important implications for Black girls' mathematics learning. One significant implication is that many white teachers resist or outright reject the inextricable links between mathematics literacy and social contexts—racial, cultural, political, and structural.[34] Therefore, there is a great need to diversify the mathematics teaching force in ways that include more Black teachers.

COMPLEXITIES OF MATHEMATICS TEACHERS DIVERSITY EFFORTS

There have been several efforts and initiatives to racially diversify the mathematics teachers' force, some of which include the National Science

Foundation's Robert Noyce Scholarship Program, Math for America, the 100Kin10, and The Black Male Mathematics Teacher Project (BM2tP).[35] The Robert Noyce Teacher Scholarship Program funds institutions of higher education to provide scholarships, stipends, and programmatic support to recruit and prepare STEM majors and professionals to become K–12 teachers in high-needs school districts. High-needs schools often have a larger percentage of Black students; thus, this program has some potential for exposing Black girls to more Black mathematics teachers.

One example of a Noyce program with much potential for exposing Black young women to more Black mathematics teachers is the Vanderbilt-Fisk Noyce Program, a partnership between Vanderbilt, an elite historically white institution; Fisk University, a historically Black college; and Metro Nashville Public schools, all located in Nashville, Tennessee.[36] First, Fisk is a majority Black institution with women making up 70 percent of its students.[37] Fisk also has a strong reputation for producing outstanding Black women graduates, both historically and currently, some of whom include Ida B. Wells, Johnnetta B. Cole, and Nikki Giovanni.[38] Further, with its varied selection of more than twenty undergraduate STEM-related programs, including mathematics, biology, chemistry, and physics, Fisk is surely an institution where Black young women are encouraged to become STEM leaders and teachers.

In a 2019 study that I conducted with Heather Johnson and Teresa Dunleavy, the directors of the Vanderbilt-Fisk Noyce Program, we found that Fisk in fact is a place where Black women are exposed to science and teaching.[39] In an interview, Ramona, a Fisk student and graduate, described a proud narrative: "Put me up against any university, HBCU or PWI. Put me up against them. Fisk stands tall . . . We stand firm in the scholars we produce, second to none, we produce them."[40] She also praised the opportunity she had to participate in a Fisk-sponsored afterschool science program for middle school girls, which helped her decide to become a teacher. The outreach program director, Mr. Abraham, identified Ramona's teaching talents and encouraged her to go through the Noyce Program at Vanderbilt, which contributed to a pivot in her professional trajectory from a bench biologist to a secondary school science teacher. Ramona's identity as a Black woman who always loved science helped her to establish rapport and relationships with her middle school students in that program. She stated: "I realized every single time I needed a pick-me-up, I needed a boost where I was genuinely happy; eight times out of ten I was with my kids. No matter what."[41] This type of disposition among STEM teachers could make a difference for Black girls' science and math learning.

Yet, while recruiting and retaining more Black mathematics and science teachers is important, these efforts are complex. Black scholars have written about the myopic discourse around why more Black teachers are needed in US schools—role models, representation, and race-matching. Representation matters, but it is insufficient. For example, Toya Jones Frank, one of the trailblazing scholars who studies Black teachers of mathematics in the United States specifically, posits that emphasizing the need to diversify the mathematics teaching force for the sole purpose of race-matching does no more than commodify these teachers.[42] While this call to recruit and retain Black teachers promotes potential role-modeling through race-matching as a tactic for improving Black students' growth and achievement, historically racist hiring and teaching practices that undervalue Black teachers and maintain the status quo in mathematics education remain unchallenged.[43]

Black racial discrimination in teacher hiring is not new. *Brown v. Board of Education of Topeka* was a landmark 1954 Supreme Court case in which the justices ruled unanimously that racial segregation of children in public schools was unconstitutional. But *Brown* also had an unintended consequence, the effects of which are still felt today. The landmark case caused the dismissal, demotion, or forced resignation of many experienced, highly credentialed Black educators who staffed Black-only schools. After the decision, tens of thousands of Black teachers and principals lost their jobs as white superintendents began to integrate schools but outright rejected hiring Black educators in positions of authority over white teachers or students.[44]

A more contemporary example is the 2010 *Moore v. Tangipahoa Parish School Board* case in Louisiana. A court reopened the 1965 school desegregation case in 2006, and then in 2010, a judge issued a new desegregation plan that applied specialized teacher-hiring criteria that gave extensive preference to Black teachers.[45] School principals were required to select a qualified Black applicant if they applied for a vacant teaching position, and if a Black applicant was in the pool but not chosen, the principal would be required to submit written reasons for the choice to a district committee.[46] The researchers who examined this desegregation case found that the impact of the court-ordered hiring reform did in fact increase the share of teachers who are Black in this particular district relative to the rest of the state.[47] Another consequence of this policy was a decrease in the student-teacher representation gap—defined as the difference in enrollment share among Black students and teachers in a district, as well as an increase in the share of Black teachers holding positions in both predominately white and predominately Black schools in the Tangipahoa Parish School district.[48] An important question to ponder is, How many or what percentage of these Black teachers taught mathematics and/or science? If there were STEM teachers, how many were women? This is important to consider given what we already know about US racial and gendered narratives of STEM ability, specifically racialized and gendered narratives about Black girls and women.

Teacher diversity initiatives and efforts deepen tensions when we consider empirical studies that show causal evidence that Black students who have at least one Black teacher in elementary school are 9 percentage points (13 percent) more likely to graduate from high school and 6 percentage points (19 percent) more likely to enroll in college than their peers who are not assigned to a Black teacher.[49] The Tennessee STAR study built on other studies that showed mounting evidence that same-race teachers are beneficial to underrepresented minority students on a number of dimensions, such as test scores, attendance, course grades, disciplinary outcomes, and expectations in a variety of educational settings.[50] Considering the extensive body of literature on the exclusionary discipline outcomes among Black girls, the Tennessee STAR study's findings are important. Specifically, they have potential for supporting policies and practices that can shape long-term positive effects and outcomes of Black girls when they have Black teachers.

Overall, what we learn from the teacher diversity discourse is that the lack of racial diversity in the American public school system, and mathematics teachers specifically, is rooted in a long legacy of inequality. The system is fraught with multifaceted issues, and the key takeaway is that role models, representation, and race-making have some merit, but those discourses must be problematized with the inequitable structural factors in the education system, as well as with research findings about recruitment and retention experiences of Black mathematics teachers. Doing so will provide a more nuanced picture of what policy makers should consider when creating reforms for teacher diversity.

An important scholar who studies reform in teacher diversity, Linda Darling-Hammond, explored with colleagues—Black teachers generally, and Black women teachers specifically—why they leave the profession and what it would take to get them back. Their recommendations, which add to the conversation about Black teachers and diversity efforts, suggested that for targeted policy interventions, a focus on teacher residencies, loan forgiveness, mentoring and induction, and principal training programs is necessary.[51] The implications for teaching and teacher education are significant when considering *who has the right to teach mathematics to Black girls.* The current reality is that white women are more than likely educating Black girls in K–12 classrooms. We also know that diversity efforts aim to recruit more Black teachers for Black students to have more role models and see themselves in their teachers; however, these efforts are often shortsighted, and the need for sociocultural and sociopolitical knowledge often goes unnoticed in large-scale policy work.[52]

DEVELOPING MATHEMATICS TEACHERS' CAPACITY FOR ONGOING, CRITICAL SELF-WORK

Given the realities and tensions regarding teacher diversity and educating Black girls, I return to my recommendation of a transformative action plan for teachers; both in-service and preservice is necessary. This is a plan that can be constructed "on Monday"; teachers need not wait for legislation or policy to tell them what needs to be done to develop into excellent teachers of mathematics for Black girls.[53] Remember that this chapter is for mathematics teachers who are ready to go for broke. The work of teachers, general educators, researchers, and policy makers must be ongoing and intentional in designing policies and practices that address Black girls' robust mathematics development and achievement.

One way to do this work is for mathematics teachers to engage in writing their own transformative plans of action that include three areas. These three features are not mutually exclusive but work in tandem to serve as a daily reminder to the teacher of their goals and action steps. Examining their goals on a regular basis can also serve as a reminder of "how" and "why" they are qualified to teach rigorous mathematics for liberation and human flourishing to Black girls.[54] Teaching mathematics in ways that inspire Black girl joy and liberation calls for radical change of the current systems, policies, and practices. Writing a transformative plan is one way to do the work; we know that in teaching, flexibility is key. It is meant to be revisited in iterative ways that allow for adjustments as needed. Further, this plan is not a panacea. This plan addresses the work of teaching but does not necessarily mitigate other challenges Black girls face in mathematics education. The core of writing a transformative plan or doing any work related to supporting Black girls' mathematics literacies is critical consciousness. Mathematics education researcher Danny Martin poignantly stated, "Effective teaching is not just about having a powerful command of the content that you teach. Who you are, who you teach, and under what sociocultural, sociopolitical, and sociostructural conditions are equally important and will heavily influence how you teach and toward what ends."[55] And in Martin's perspective, teachers should remember that these features will look different given one's positionality and, at various times, some features may be emphasized more than others. The goal is to stick with the critical self-reflective work and never give up. The following sections outline the three features that should be present in any transformative plan that is pursuing liberatory mathematics education for Black girls.

1: TRANSFORMATIVE TEACHERS OF MATHEMATICS UNDERSTAND HOW CRITICAL RACIAL IDENTITY DEVELOPMENT DIVESTS FROM WHITENESS

The first feature of the transformative action plan is racial identity development work for teachers of mathematics. Racial identity development helps one to understand the range of views, concepts, and emotions that people experience over time about their racial identity. Black psychologists, such as William Cross and Bailey Jackson III, advanced early Black racial identity development models in the 1970s.[56] Janet Helms later built upon Cross's model to think about white racial identity. Helms identified six stages in which white people can find themselves at any time.[57]

> *Stage 1. Contact*: Obliviousness to own racial identity
> *Stage 2. Disintegration*: First acknowledgment of white identity
> *Stage 3. Reintegration*: Idealizes whites/denigrates (people of color)
> *Stage 4. Pseudo-independence*: Intellectualized acceptance of own and others' race
> *Stage 5. Immersion/emersion*: Honest appraisal of racism and significance of white identity
> *Stage 6. Autonomy*: Internalizes a multicultural identity with nonracist white identity as its core

Transformative teachers of mathematics who have the right to teach Black girls are in stage six because those teachers understand themselves and their Black girls as *racial beings in a racialized society* that requires acting to form a healthy white racial identity, which Helms defines as an anti-racist identity. Similarly, teachers of color should also interrogate whiteness and work to develop a healthy racial identity. Transformative teachers of mathematics own a clear anti-racist and abolitionist teacher identity and consistently interrogate whiteness, meaning they recognize how various forms of racism—institutionalized, cultural, and individual—benefit white people, and they seek ways to interrupt this system.[58] One important way of disruption is to educate other mathematics teachers, general educators, family members, friends, and Black girls to identify, name, and challenge the norms, patterns, traditions, structures, and institutions that keep racism and white supremacy in place.[59] Because teachers' racial identities are intricately intertwined with the way they teach and with the relationships they have with their students, transformative teachers of mathematics (TToM) do not question the relevance and importance of this critical self-work.[60] TToM have developed the knowledge of systems of oppression, privilege, inequity, and identity within the US mathematics education system and make decisions about curriculum, pedagogies, how to interact with Black girls, and other important choices that consider these sociopolitical realities.

What this can look like is using a tool called *critical reflexivity*, which asks teachers to examine how they are shaped by the social, cultural, political, and economic forces within the context of teaching mathematics as well as their own roles in shaping those contexts.[61] Scholars of teacher identity point out that preservice and in-service teachers of mathematics benefit from such attention to identity work. Jenelle Reeves contends that critical reflexivity requires teachers to examine not only societal or institutional inequities, but also their own implications in those inequities via their teacher identity and the positions they may inhabit.[62] For example, writing teachers' life history narratives can help teachers identify, through written and oral reflection, the cultural resources and constraints that arise from their personal and social histories.[63] These activities could be assignments in teacher education programs as well as summer work for teachers already in the workforce. Again, this work should be done in community with other like-minded teachers.

For teachers to deeply reflect their teacher identities within educational institutions, they need to look at society, schools, and policies with a skeptical, inquiring eye. This is imperative because society, schools, and educational policies are socially negotiated and imbued with vested interests and power inequities that uphold whiteness and white supremacy. TToM do the work to imagine alternative identities that often leads to the creation of new, different instructional practices that are liberatory and social-justice oriented for Black girls' mathematics development, participation, and ultimately achievement. Disrupting teachers established societal or institutional assumptions and ways of being is key to opening teachers' imagination to alternative perspectives on who they can be as teachers.

Toward that end, immersing mathematics teachers who are ready to go for broke, through field experiences, in a new school setting with new institutional ways of being is one promising strategy. Another idea, given shortages and the constraints of schooling, could include mathematics teachers teaching across the mathematics course offerings. This exposes the math teachers to different demographics of students, thus giving them a wider view and perspective of not only the structural inequalities Black girls face in their mathematics education, but potentially promising practices that support Black girls. This teacher exchange program could start locally within one school, then build out across schools both in and out of larger districts and even cross-country initiatives. Without an understanding of how teacher identities are negotiated—the push and pull of internal and external forces—teachers may be hampered in finding and using their own agency to claim healthy and productive teacher identity positions.

2: TRANSFORMATIVE TEACHERS OF MATHEMATICS UNDERSTAND BLACK GIRLHOOD

The second component of the transformative action plan is understanding and appreciating Black girlhood in all its complexity and diversity, at both the structural and interpersonal levels. James Baldwin pointed out in his 1963 speech that Black people who are born in the United States and go through the educational system run the risk of becoming unsettled, because on one hand, the United States promotes liberty and justice for all and promotes itself as the richest country with plenty of opportunities for its citizens to be successful. Yet on the other hand, Black people are assured by society, teachers, administrators, and other adults in their lives that they do not matter.

Black girlhood is situated in Black life. Aria S. Halliday discussed how, through the imaginings of early autobiographical work by Black women in North America such as Zora Neal Hurston, Jamaica Kincaid, Phyllis Wheatley, bell hooks, and others:

> We see the world as Black girls do—a world that is violent, dehumanizing, disrespectful, and hateful towards girls whose hair puffs, whose full lips part to make way for a big smile and a belly laugh, whose voices rise and fall with the heartiness of ancestors, and whose skin glistens like gold when caught in sunlight.[64]

Halliday argues that while Black women have worked to create spaces for Black girls in academic discussions of education, history, literacy, community work, and the future, Black girls have been subsumed within Black women's theorizing, which essentially suggests that this has adultified Black girls. To adultify a Black girl is to rob her of her innocence, and many teachers rob Black girls of clemency—in dress codes, no-excuses policies, and other policies and practices that harm Black girls. A groundswell of Black girlhood scholars has engaged in Black girlhood theorizing to unpack what it means to be a Black girl in schools and society. Some of those scholars include Ruth Nicole Brown, Aimee Meredith Cox, Venus Evans-Winters, Monique Morris, LaKisha Simons, and Dominique Hill.[65] In her foundational text, "Hear Our Truths: The Creative Potential of Black Girls," Ruth Nicole Brown's first words on the page are:

> The vision: Black girlhood is freedom, and Black girls are free. As an organizing construct, Black girlhood makes possible the affirmation of Black girls' lives and, if necessary, their liberation. Black girlhood as a spatial intervention is useful for making our daily lives better and therefore changing the world as we currently know it. Love guides our actions and permeates our beings. For those who do not know love, we create spaces to practice Black girlhood and sense love, to name it, claim it, and share it. What we know, what we say, our process, and what we make is of value, especially if it surfaces in unexpected forms. The space is specific enough that Black girls recognize it as theirs. The making of the space is collective and creative, uncertainty and complexity motivate, and revolutionary action is a goal. [66]

This vision is beautiful and positions Black girls as worthy of knowing in deep and complex ways. Mathematics teachers who are ready to go for broke should read these texts to develop new imaginations of Black girlhood that resist racialized and gendered stereotypes—loud, sassy, and overly sexual. Concrete examples could include a teacher-student book club that invites Black girls to read about positive and complex narratives of Black girls as well as inviting them to share their own stories of mathematics learning in their trajectories. Mathematics teachers could also invite and nurture Black girls' gesturing and language in the classroom as tools for understanding mathematics content.

Recently, scholars have suggested that Black English is one possible entry into culturally relevant mathematics, since we know that discourse and language are inherently significant aspects of learning mathematics.[67] Inviting other mathematics teachers to be a part of these learning exercises could also be powerful. Activities do not have be major projects. The point is to create spaces for co-constructing and learning together. Teachers who are ready to go for broke show their vulnerability and openness for acknowledging that Black girls are the experts in the room and that their expertise in their Black girlhood can shed light on how to change some of the social realities they face in mathematics classrooms and schools. Choosing to see Black girls in this light and to care enough about what you see to act is a TToM move. Humanizing and respectful relationships with Black girls are possible with this type of commitment by their mathematics teachers.

3: TRANSFORMATIVE TEACHERS OF MATHEMATICS CRITICALLY REFLECT ON THEIR INSTRUCTION AND PEDAGOGIES

Chapter 4 used Black girl narratives and perspectives to unpack the types of pedagogies that supported their mathematics learning and development in classrooms. But again, because we know that US society believes that Black people and girls, generally, cannot be successful in mathematics, focusing on Black girls and how mathematics teachers instruct them is crucial. It is widely understood that teachers are often overwhelmed with expectations about preparing their students to pass standardized assessments and other outcomes. School schedules are also often organized with little room for teachers to use the restroom, let alone engage in critical reflection about their mathematics instruction. But many mathematics teachers find ways to do this work, which requires being intentional and committed to improving instruction for Black girls.

To critically reflect is to think at the intersection of content knowledge and Black girlhood, because the two are integral for TToM who want to develop Black girls' mathematics literacies. Videotaping one's teaching and then using that footage to zoom in how Black girls experienced the mathematics lesson and instruction is just one way to critically reflect on teacher practice. Watching Deborah Ball's presentation about discretionary space and Black girlhood could be a concrete example for what it means to critically reflect at the intersection of mathematics content knowledge and Black girlhood.[68] In a one-minute twenty-eight-second period that was filmed in her classroom, Ball counted twenty separate micro moments when she had to decide how to react. She calls them "discretionary spaces," and in a lecture at the American Educational Research Association's annual meeting in April 2018, she put a scientist's microscope on discretionary space nineteen to illuminate how racism and sexism exists in the classroom and the teaching of mathematics. For example, a micro-moment at the intersection of mathematics teaching and Black girlhood could include reframing a Black girls' question to another student that may appear on the surface as disrespectful as a Black cultural communication style known as signifying.[69]

The trained eye would know that signification is a way of saying something on two different levels at once; it can be used to send a message of social critique and is often done in a direct way. This is very different from white culture, for example, and it should not be viewed as deficient. TToM with a deep understanding of Black girlhood take as axiomatic that Black girls are brilliant. Ball points out that when mathematics teachers start from that premise, they can see the mathematical knowledge that Black girls bring to sense-making of various mathematics concepts.

TToM critically reflecting in the public space with other like-minded teachers are important for modeling and being held accountable to the work. This also provides opportunities to share methodologies of mathematics instruction among teachers, especially if those strategies are proving to be effective with Black girls. "Effective" is a loaded term, so *Making Black Girls Count in Math Education* views effective in this case as an increase of Black girls' sense of belonging in mathematics, which can increase her motivation to participate. Effective also means that a Black girl's participation grows over time to communicate her math ideas, uses appropriate vocabulary (conversational/formal) in that communication process, takes risks to try harder mathematics problems, constructs questions about mathematics ideas, and demonstrates her learning through different types of assessments. Effective means that her mathematics identities get stronger—she has interest in mathematics, she views herself as a mathematician, she regularly gets recognized as a mathematical thinker, and she feels confident and competent in her ability to perform mathematically in the classroom. Finally, effective means that a Black girl understands that her informal mathematical knowledge in learning school mathematics is an important resource that is welcomed in the formal classroom. TToM need to create collegial norms and practices that support such public reflection and investigation.[70]

CONCLUSION

James Baldwin said in his 1963 speech that the purpose of education is to create in a person the ability to look at the world for themselves and make their own decisions, and that to ask questions of the universe and then learn to live with those questions is the way people achieve their own identity. Black girls seldom have these opportunities to question and resist identities that educators in schools have placed on them. Mathematics teachers have also contributed to this mischaracterization of Black girls. Thus, the work of unlearning and rejecting these identities is solidarity work that mathematics teachers must first begin with the interrogation of the self. This chapter specifically is speaking to mathematics teachers who want to stop making excuses and blaming Black girls and their families for low mathematics achievement.

Because most mathematics teachers are white, and research suggests that racial-matching between students and teachers has important benefits, many efforts among organizations to increase racial diversity in the mathematics teacher force are popular. But it is important to problematize racial-matching rationales for increasing Black students' mathematics achievement. A focus on recruitment and retention is critical to expand the conversation about issues Black mathematics teachers face in their careers. But in the meantime, and simultaneously, working with the system we have is meaningful, so this chapter introduced a three-concept plan for mathematics teachers who want to develop into outstanding instructors for Black girls. Setting ongoing goals around the importance of teacher racial identities, Black girlhood, and critical reflection of mathematics instruction sets up mathematics teachers to do their work differently. It is not a silver-bullet answer; it is, however, a starting point for mathematics teachers who are ready to go for broke in solidarity with Black girls.

WHERE DO WE GO FROM HERE?

Making Black Girls Count in Mathematics Education

*M*aking Black Girls Count in Math Education aims to do three things. First, it provides an overall critique of mathematics education research, practice, and policy for neglecting Black girls and women. The critique invokes intersectional theories to both historicize and highlight their invisibility in ways that made these issues bear weight to the uncritical eye. Today, while we have a burgeoning level of research and scholarship, the field needs more—and that more should not be single axis, but intersectional. Some scholars have examined cognition, achievement, and other metric constructs among Black girls by using them for a comparison group, usually to white students, or the research examines lines of inquiry through race (African American students) or gender (girls), leaving Black girls and women hidden in plain sight. There is also a need for additional critical quantitative research to better understand the "what" that is happening with Black girls and women at every level.

Second, *Making Black Girls Count in Math Education* situates Black girls' experiences in various contexts—learning environments, mathematics curriculum, pedagogies, formative and summative assessments, and teacher education. These chapters illuminate problematic experiences, but also provide remedies for how to change these contexts to better support Black girls and women. Being transparent about these negative issues is important because the average person does not have the privilege of conducting research and asking such questions that allow for interrogation and analysis. Thus, what happens is that everyday families and society have a one-sided perspective of Black girls and women as it relates to their mathematics education (i.e., access, participation, achievement) and these perspectives are oftentimes uncritical, without complexity. Thus, *Making Black Girls Count in Math Education* disrupts the naive thinking about Black girls' and women's mathematics education in US society. Mathematics teaching and learning are political endeavors, meaning they are shaped by broader issues, such as who teaches mathematics to Black girls, what kind of curriculum the teachers use, what mathematics teachers believe about Black girls and their families broadly, and what type of learning experiences mathematics teachers think Black girls deserve and need. Society would have us think that mathematics is neutral, numbers are numbers, and race and gender have nothing to do with learning mathematics. But the reality is that when we do not politicize Black girls' mathematics access, learning, development, participation, and achievement, we leave hegemony and white supremacy undisputed, which always provides a single story, not a nuanced narrative.

Finally, *Making Black Girls Count in Math Education* invites coalition building among teachers, educators, families, policy makers, Black girls, and other relevant stakeholders because this is shared, difficult, and lifelong work. It is everyone's responsibility to address and transform these issues. Structures, systems, ideologies, and practices do not change with one outstanding person doing the work; they change with hundreds and thousands of individuals taking a piece of the work, going as deep as possible, and acting in transformative and humanizing ways. Paulo Freire points out that we must have critical consciousness to do liberatory work. Taking up space for Black girls in mathematics contexts will require that one be critically consciousness about whiteness, white supremacy, race, racism, Black girlhood, and many other interlocking systems of oppression in our society and schools.[1] If individuals are not interested in interrogating these systems in relationship to mathematics, they are not doing authentic equity work. Rochelle Gutierrez pointed out that an equity approach through access and achievement only, without examinations of power and identity, is shortsighted and limited.[2] Overall, my hope is that *Making Black Girls Count in Math Education* inspires catalytic and radical change in service of every little Black girl in this nation and world.

KEY THEMES

In the spirit of making this book accessible to several audiences, I offer the following are five big ideas that readers should take away:

- The US mathematics education system (i.e., culture, discourse, policies, and practices) does not love Black girls. It has been intentionally designed to erase their humanities and dehumanize them. When mathematics teachers focus on identifying Black girls as too loud and talkative, rather than identifying them for gifted programming or teaching them through ambitious instruction, they disqualify themselves to teach Black girls.
- Chronic negative experiences such as low teacher expectations, internalization of Black girl stereotypes among teachers, mathematics worksheets, limited opportunities for group work and socialization, uninteresting curriculum, and sparse early and consistent exposure to conceptual learning contribute to Black girls' underrepresentation, fragmented identities, and overall pushout of mathematics and STEM.
- The US mathematics education system is structurally exclusionary, oppressive, and upholds gendered anti-Blackness and white supremacy. Nothing is neutral or impartial about the US mathematics education system. Thus, there will always be a counter story about racialized and gendered experiences among Black girls that complicates the "mathematics for all" rhetoric.
- Mathematics teachers, both pre- and in-service, have no structural incentive to change or do what is right for Black girls. Professional development in K–12 in critically examining one's teaching and how teaching practices shape Black girls' learning outcomes is essentially nonexistent. Additionally, many university mathematics professors, especially those who are tenured, will probably never change because some view

their recommendation to a Black girl to "drop this class if you cannot keep up" as a protective factor, not a reinforcement of racial-gendered oppression or white benevolence.[3]

- Every Black girl can learn mathematics. Every Black girl has the capacity to learn mathematics and deserves to be taught mathematics in comprehensible ways.

WHERE DO WE GO FROM HERE? WHAT BLACK GIRLS NEED

As a Black girl cartographer, it is important for me to think at the intersection of research and practice. The following is a list of recommendations that I shared at an invited talk at the National Academies of Science, Engineering, and Medicine on June 20, 2021. I suggested that these recommendations be carried out in solidarity with Black girls and their families; otherwise, we run the risk of perpetuating current inequalities.

Black girls need funding agencies (national, state, local, private, non-profit, philanthropic, federal) to establish ongoing and significant support for projects focused on Black girls' and women's experiences and outcomes in mathematics and STEM broadly.

Black girls need racially conscious mathematics instructors who share power, make the curriculum interesting and challenging, build caring and authentic relationships with students, hold high expectations, and allow humor and fun. Black girls need their racially conscious mathematics instructors to also have strong content knowledge and use a mathematics curriculum that is inquiry-based, rigorous, and culturally relevant. Consequently, teachers should stop using worksheets as a main instructional activity. Robust pedagogies can include problem posing, classroom discourse, small group work, and manipulatives and technology for modeling mathematical ideas.

Black girls need school systems and the people who work there to treat them with dignity, understanding that they are complex individuals who have a right to bring their full humanities to learning spaces and contexts. *Black girls need* strong cultural brokers and advocates for accessing educational resources, such as recommendations for gifted and talented programs, summer STEM programs, and paid internships.

Black girls need policies that create opportunities for "intersectional interventions." An example of an intersectional intervention would be a "Black Girls Do Mathematics Club" at a local school or community organization. The club would be advised and facilitated preferably by a critically conscious Black woman mathematics instructor because representation matters. Representation is insufficient, but it matters. *Black girls need* university-level mathematics professors to reject the idea of neutrality of mathematics learning but understand the role that racialized and gendered oppression has played in preventing many Black women from feeling like they belong in mathematics, which can push them out of STEM.

FUTURE RESEARCH AGENDA: WAYS TO PUT "BLACK GIRLS' NEEDS" INTO ACTION

What we know about most funding agencies, whether private or public, large or small, is that they desire to fund research and scholarship that is compelling, fills gaps in the literature, and be large scale if possible. One future line of inquiry is large-scale local and national quantitative studies that document the "what" for Black girls' experiences in mathematics, STEM, or schooling in general. The National Center for Educational Statistics has several data sets available to researchers, including the Civil Rights Data Collection (CRDC). The CRDC collects a variety of information including student enrollment and educational programs and services, most of which is disaggregated by race or ethnicity, gender, limited English proficiency, and disability. The CRDC is a long-standing and important aspect of the overall strategy of the Office for Civil Rights for administering and enforcing the civil rights statutes for which it is responsible. The data it collects is often used by other US Department of Education offices, as well as policy makers.

One important data set it collects is mathematics and science course enrollment among African American students across the country. While these large data sets are useful, the survey questions are already constructed and cannot be changed, so researchers or educators might think about designing their own surveys to get at important questions useful for their local context. For example, some local research questions could be "What percentage of Black girls are in gifted/talented programs at our school and in our larger school district?" and "What percentage of Black girls are in remedial and/or lower-level mathematics courses?" These are questions that would not necessarily need a survey unless that data were not readily available via in-house databases. What might be the case is the discovery that this type of data is not even collected, which could be a signal that perhaps such questions are not a concern of the school and educators.

Making a commitment to begin collecting such data to inform local decisions and policies would be beneficial in acting through an access lens for equity. But further questions such as "How does our school or district decide on gifted/talented identification? Who decided the identification process would be this way? Why doesn't the process change if it consistently omits large percentages of Black girls?" would need to be answered to engage in thinking about power as an approach to equity. These questions examine who holds power to make these decisions and who benefits from current rules and policies. Using these findings to make different decisions and create more inclusive policies is an example of putting what Black girls need into action. Sharing these findings with Black girls' families in the spirit of transparency could prove transformative, especially if these courageous conversations include the codevelopment of a plan to address the findings. Schools and communities working together in authentic and meaningful ways strengthen connections and relationships.

Other important questions that need exploring include "What key factors propel the success of Black girls and women in mathematics, and do these factors change over time?" "What are Black girls' and women's strategies of persistence and resistance in mathematics learning?" "What noninstitutionalized mathematics practices do Black girls and women engage in in their everyday lives, and how, if at all, have these informal practices supported their learning of formal mathematics?" "What types of mathematics instruction are early childhood Black girls exposed to in their classrooms?" Additional research and scholarship that envisions and creates mathematics educational spaces that are structured to understand and foster Black girls' flourishing are sorely needed. Counternarratives rooted in Black girls' brilliance in mathematics as axiomatic pushes back and disrupts current knowledge steeped in the white gaze.[4]

Finally, there is a need for the development of scholarship that examines the mathematics experiences of Black girls and women grounded on robust understandings of historical and sociopolitical configurations that impact their experiences inside and outside mathematics. My colleagues Dr. Toya Jones Frank, Taqiyyah Elliot, and I published a paper calling for a critical historical perspective when examining mathematics education issues for Black communities.[5]

WHAT CAN TEACHERS DO NOW? WHAT ABOUT MONDAY?

Supporting Black girls' mathematics development and achievement need not wait for the radical dismantling of the current mathematics education system. There are evidence-based practices that a teacher can start implementing on Monday.[6] Teachers can decide to practice an ethic of care and liberation by being more attentive to the Black girls in their classes, responding positively to their Black girls' expressed needs.[7] Black girls often seek a connection with their teachers, so working to develop authentic relationships built on respect and trust is necessary. Taking this step might require certain teachers to apologize to specific Black girls in their classrooms. They need to apologize and acknowledge that Black girls are not supported, but that they are taking steps to do things differently. Having the attention of a Black girl is more likely when she knows that her teachers are authentic.

Math teachers can choose to start journaling about their Black girls on Monday to engage in some critical reflection, asking themselves questions such as, "What do I really believe about Black girls? Where did I develop those beliefs? What type of things have I done to support them? How do I know if the things that I did were supportive? What things have I done to harm them? How do I know it harmed the Black girl?" Based on the responses to these questions, teachers can choose one thing to work on for a few weeks, evaluate, and start again.

Mathematics teachers can decide to do content and pedagogical interviews with some of their Black girls on Monday. For example, whatever content or topic is currently being engaged in, the interviews can focus on those content questions and include questions about their experiences of the learning. Asking "What are you feeling good about with learning X?" "What seems to come easy and why?" "What is hard and how do you know?" can give mathematics teachers insight into the math learning of their Black girls, which can lead to unlearning or dismantling any deficit ideologies or thinking about Black girls. These types of interactions can also help the teachers see that Black girls are indeed invested in their learning.

On Monday, mathematics teachers can start providing high-quality instruction that de-emphasizes rote memorization and facilitates conceptual understanding, procedural flexibility, strategic competence, adaptive reasoning, and productive dispositions.[8] These experiences align with state standards for mathematical practices. For a mathematics teacher to de-emphasize some of these procedural methodologies, carefully considering how often and how effectively worksheets are in their lessons for deep learning is a good first step.[9] Black girls need and want challenging work that includes authentic tasks and interesting problems. Other ideas for high-quality instruction include teachers integrating more class discussions and group work to foster more active learning among their Black girls.[10] Teachers can also start being more intentional about connecting some of their content to life outside the class, including career applications.[11] A study that I conducted with two Joseph Mathematics Education Research Lab (JMEL) members found that the high school Black girls in the study did not see how the mathematics they were learning prepared them for the wonderful future careers they all identified, including professions like dentist, veterinarian, and hair salon owner.[12] One idea about facilitating more conceptual understanding is for teachers to be prepared and willing to compare and explain multiple strategies for problem solving, and some of those problems could be related to STEM careers.[13] Finally, teachers can start using more formative assessments to better understand what Black girls know and are able to do (see chapter 5 for detailed discussion).

Overall, there is much work to do, and while the US mathematics education system is wrought with inequalities and seeks to simply reproduce educational experiences for Black girls that develop them into consumers instead of knowledge producers, we must stay in the struggle. In the final section, I draw on bell hooks' idea of "sisterhood and political solidarity between women" to develop one component of resistance to the broader ideologies, discourses, policies, and practices that undermine Black girls' development across mathematics trajectories.[14] This is a call to society and the field.

BLACK WOMEN'S SISTERHOOD IN SERVICE OF BLACK GIRLS' MATHEMATICS FLOURISHING

Dismantling and disrupting ideologies, discourse, policies, and practices that undermine Black girls' development across mathematics trajectories is no small feat. As already discussed throughout the text, mathematics is a historically white and masculine field with deep norms rooted in white supremacy culture, such as innateness of mathematical ability or mathematics as apolitical in social contexts. Another challenge of dismantling and disrupting discourses, ideologies, and practices that undermine Black girls' thriving in mathematics is how some Black women, who have benefited from the current system, are socialized to behave in ways that make them act in complicity with the status quo.[15] For example, in his analysis of undergraduate Black women's narratives of their experiences navigating P–16 mathematics, Luis Leyva found that the Black women in his study (Bia, Kim, and Sierra) internalized racial-gendered ideologies about math ability and normalized structural inequalities in mathematics education.[16] The internalization of these commonly accepted norms in mathematics produced within-group tensions that can impede solidarity among Black women who sometimes rely on these norms to define and protect their status as mathematically successful.[17] A gripping illustration of these within-group tensions of divisiveness between Black women came from Bia, an African woman with immigration history and a computer science major. In her interview, Bia stated:

> In chemistry class, there is me and two other African American girls.
> I don't know why they just didn't talk to me, and I didn't talk to them. I
> never had anything against them, *but they just helped themselves* [emphasis

added], helped each other pass the class and I'd have to help myself and study hard on my own. *I know they did well because they bragged about how well they did* [emphasis added], but then I felt I needed to do better than them because I just have to.[18]

This narrative illuminates how Black women who have internalized logics of mathematics or STEM ability can treat other Black women. This happens because these Black women have been socialized well and benefited from competition that exists in discipline such as mathematics. hooks points out that Black women must unlearn these lessons if we are to build a sustained Black feminist movement—"We must learn to live and work in solidarity. We must learn the true meaning and value of Sisterhood."[19] And yet, although there are Black women whose internalization of white supremacy in mathematics and STEM serve as gatekeeper and oppressor to other Black women and girls, Black women disruptors also exist. This is a call for Black women in mathematics and STEM to engage in the work of long-term structural transformation in service of Black girls and women thriving in these spaces.

Black women educators with political clarity are the people we should acknowledge and gravitate toward for learning how to do the work of social justice in service of Black girls, both within and outside the classroom.[20] Therefore, Black women must take the initiative and demonstrate the power of solidarity in mathematics and STEM because solidarity strengthens resistance struggle. Black women need to protect Black girls in mathematics and STEM spaces. This protection involves serving as active allies, advocates, or co-conspirators alongside Black girls.[21] For example, in their study of Black women calculus teachers' praxis, Toya Jones Frank and colleagues featured Tangie, an Algebra II and calculus teacher.[22] Their study highlighted how Tangie regularly sought ways to bring new Black girls into the calculus pipeline but noted the structural system of tracking as a hindrance. Nonetheless, Tangie engaged in subversive strategies, as she was always on the lookout for Black girls in geometry and Algebra II who demonstrated creative and innovative ways to approach problems. Tangie also pushed against the standard identification processes that limited the participation of many Black girls in advanced mathematics.

It is well known that getting to calculus requires a particular set of prerequisite courses, but Tangie expressed that even the Black girls who met the requirements seldom made it to the course. As a result, Tangie worked against this structure and implored her fellow teachers to identify other metrics that would speak to her Black students' readiness instead of relying on traditional exclusionary methods.

Black women need to "save seats" for Black girls in mathematics and STEM spaces as a sense of belongingness.[23] There is long-standing debate about the "seat at the table" metaphor with respect to power and enacting social justice. Some suggest bringing your own chair when not invited, while others say flip the table and build something new. To tell someone that you will include them implies that they are in some way perceived as an outsider, but to tell them that they *belong* implies that they were intended to be there from the start.[24] Tangie, the calculus teacher in the study, cultivated mathematics classrooms as spaces of belonging such that Black girls knew they were always intended to fill the seats in her calculus classes. She explained, "I don't just tell my [Black] girls, 'I'll include you' . . . I tell her I was saving her seat." During her interview, she noted that she anticipated their arrival. Tangie acknowledged that Black girls in her classes often expressed isolation, which led to the desire to drop her course. As a result, Tangie learned to look for the signs that her girls may be planning to drop the course and staged one-on-one interventions that included things such as long, honest talks about the girls' concerns and Tangie's own story of persistence as a Black woman in mathematics. Overall, I am calling for Black women to lead this work in Black girls' flourishing in mathematics and STEM; these are only two examples of what it might look like in a classroom or school setting.

It would be a powerful coalition to bring together Black women STEM teachers as well as Black women in other contexts, such as executive directors of nonprofits, CEOs in the STEM industry, and governmental officials. Black women coming together in service of Black girls' flourishing and thriving in mathematics and STEM will likely mean engaging in situations where there is ideological disagreement, but bell hooks suggests that we not be afraid and do it anyway. hooks said: "This means that when women come together, rather than pretend union, we would acknowledge that we are divided and must develop strategies to overcome fears, prejudices, resentments, competitiveness, etc."[25]

Working toward sisterhood and solidarity will require that we do not shun each other but ask questions for understanding, so that real and meaningful conversations can take place. Black women need the experience of working through the hostility that STEM spaces embedded in racialized and gendered norms have created. This will free us from normalized socialization and internalized oppression, which freedom is needed to act on behalf of and with our Black girls. hooks gives us a final word of encouragement when she states:

> [Black] women do not need to eradicate differences to feel solidarity. We do not need to share common oppression to fight equally to end oppression. We do not need anti-male sentiments to bond us together, so great is the wealth of experience, culture, and ideas we have to share with one another. We can be sisters united by shared interests and beliefs, united in our appreciation for diversity, united in our struggle to end sexist oppression, united in political solidarity.[26]

This is the work that must be done in service of Black girls. The solidarity needs to be multigenerational, because this is a long game. Seats should be saved not just for you, but all the Black girls that will come after you. Also, in this work, we need to seek to better understand the Black girl imaginaries—what it looks like when no one else is in the room but Black girls. We can work together to examine what is Black girl ingenuity, self-education, and acts of protest in mathematics and STEM education contexts.

FINAL WORD AND REMINDER

I close *Making Black Girls Count in Math Education* by reminding the reader of Dr. Terri Watson's tweet—an indictment of schools, society, and mathematics education. It is also a reframing and counternarrative for Black girls' freedom.

Dear Educators,

Black girls are not loud—they want to be heard.
Black girls are not seeking attention—they are seeking a connection.
Black girls are not aggressive—they know what they want.
Black girls are not bossy—they are leaders.
Last, Black girls are not adults.

November 18, 2019

NOTES

FOREWORD

1. Robyn V. Young, *Notable Mathematicians: From Ancient Times to the Present* (Detroit: Gale Publishers, 1998).
2. Erica N. Walker, *Excellence and Devotion: Black Women in Mathematics in the United States*, in *Women in Mathematics: Celebrating the Centennial of the Mathematical Association of America*, ed. J. Beery et al. (New York: Association for Women in Mathematics and Springer, 2017), 106–20.

INTRODUCTION

1. *Making Black Girls Count: A Black Feminist Vision of Transformative Teaching* is a title that aims to show the complexities of mathematics education in the United States through the experiences of Black girls and women in mathematics and mathematics education.
2. Kimberlé Crenshaw, "Mapping the Margins: Intersectionality, Identity Politics, and Violence Against Women of Color," *Stanford Law Review* 43, no. 6 (1991): 1241–99, doi:10.2307/1229039.
3. Crenshaw, "Mapping the Margins."
4. Peter Mayo, *Liberating Praxis: Paulo Freire's Legacy for Radical Education and Politics* (Rotterdam: Sense Publishers, 2019).
5. Jamesia Thomas, "'Black Girl Magic' Is More Than a Hashtag; It's a Movement," CNN, February 24, 2016, http://www.cnn.com/2016/02/24/living/black-girl-magic-feat/; NoVo Foundation, "NoVo Foundation announces $90 million investment in girls and young women of color across the United States," press release, http://novofoundation.org/pressreleases/novo-foundation-announces-90-million-investment-ingirls-and-young-women-of-color-across-the-united-states/.
6. "Black Girl Freedom Fund: Extraordinary Times Require Extraordinary Measures," *Essence*, December 6, 2020, https://www.essence.com/feature/1-billion-4-black-girls-freedom-fund/.
7. "Black Girl Freedom Fund," second paragraph.
8. Maisie Gholson and Danny B. Martin, "Smart Girls, Black Girls, Mean Girls, and Bullies: At the Intersection of Identities and the Mediating Role of Young

Girls' Social Networks in Mathematical Communities of Practice," *Journal of Education* 194, no. 1 (2014): 19–33; Nicole M. Joseph, Meseret Hailu, and Denise Boston, "Black Girls' and Women's Persistence in the P–20 Mathematics Pipeline: Two Decades of Children and Youth Education Research," *Review of Research* (in press); Nicole M. Joseph, Chayla M. Haynes, and Floyd Cobb, eds., *Interrogating Whiteness and Relinquishing Power: White Faculty's Commitment to Racial Consciousness in STEM Classrooms* (New York: Peter Lang, 2016); Patricia C. Kenschaft, "Black women in mathematics in the United States," *American Mathematical Monthly* 88 (1981): 592–604; Danny B. Martin, "Learning mathematics while Black," *Journal of Educational Foundations* 26, no. 1/2 (2012): 47–66; Erika N. Walker, *Beyond Banneker: Black Mathematicians and the Paths to Excellence* (Albany: SUNY Press, 2014).

9. Luis A. Leyva, "Black Women's Counter-stories of Resilience and Within-group Tensions in the White, Patriarchal Space of Mathematics Education," *Journal for Research in Mathematics Education* 52, no. 2 (forthcoming).

10. Carter G. Woodson, *The Miseducation of the Negro* (New York: Associated Press, 1933).

11. Woodson, *The Miseducation of the Negro,* 75.

12. Woodson, *The Miseducation of the Negro,* 75.

13. Abbe H. Herzig, "Becoming Mathematicians: Women and Students of Color Choosing and Leaving Doctoral Mathematics," *Review of Educational Research* 74, no. 2 (2004): 171–214; Sara N. Hottinger, *Inventing the Mathematician: Gender, Race, and our Cultural Understanding of Mathematics* (Albany: SUNY Press, 2016).

14. bell hooks, *Talking Back: Thinking Feminist, Thinking Black* (Boston: South End Press, 1989). Talking back is rooted in Black culture whereby if one "talked back," it meant speaking as an equal to an authority figure. To speak when not spoken to was an act of courage because it meant punishment. Engaging in back talk is what hooks attributes to the finding of her authentic voice. She writes as an act of resistance.

15. Adam Fairclough, A *Class of Their Own: Black Teachers in the Segregated South* (Cambridge, MA: Harvard University Press, 2009), 40.

16. Margot Lee Shetterly, *Hidden Figures: The American Dream and the Untold Story of the Black Women Mathematicians Who Helped Win the Space Race* (New York: HarperCollins, 2016), xiii.

17. Shetterly, *Hidden Figures.,* xiii.

18. Shetterly, *Hidden Figures,* xiii.

19. Nicole M. Joseph et al., "What Plato Took for Granted: Examining the Biographies of the First Five African American Female Mathematicians and What that Says About Resistance to the Western Epistemological Cannon," in *Women of Color in STEM: Navigating the Workforce,* eds. Julia Ballenger, Barbara Polnick, and Beverly Irby (Charlotte, NC: Information Age Publishing, 2016), 3–38.

20. Joseph et al., "What Plato Took for Granted," 27.

21. Vivienne Malone Mayes, *Black and Female* (Princeton, NJ: Princeton University Press, 2005). Dr. Vivienne Malone-Mayes stated: "When you are both

Black and a female, it is difficult to distinguish which of these traits may account for the way you are received by others. I shall briefly review my career as a student and as a professor in an attempt to use hindsight as a tool in determining the influence these traits may have had on my professional growth. In many instances, it will be quite difficult to conclude whether these events happened because I am Black or because I am a woman or because I am both Black and female"; Ebony O. McGee and Danny B. Martin, "'You would not believe what I have to go through to prove my intellectual value!' Stereotype Management Among Academically Successful Black Mathematics and Engineering students," *American Educational Research Journal* 48, no. 6 (2011): 1347–89.

22. Nicole M. Joseph, Meseret Hailu, and Denise Boston, "Black Girls' and Women's Persistence in the P–20 Mathematics Pipeline: Two Decades of Children and Youth Education Research," *Review of Research* (in press); Patricia C. Kenschaft, "Black Women in Mathematics in the United States," *American Mathematical Monthly* 88, (1981): 592–604; *Beyond Banneker.*

23. Walker, *Beyond Banneker,* 3.

24. Tamara T. Butler, "Black Girl Cartography: Black Girlhood and Place-making in Education Research," *Review of Research in Education* 42, no. 1 (2018): 28–45; Richard Delgado, "Rodrigo's Reconsideration: Intersectionality and the Future of Critical Race Theory," *Iowa Law Review* 96 (2010): 1247; Cynthia B. Dillard, "The Substance of Things Hoped for, the Evidence of Things Not Seen: Examining an Endarkened Feminist Epistemology in Educational Research and Leadership," *International Journal of Qualitative Studies in Education* 13, no. 6 (2000): 661–81.

25. Chayla Haynes et al., "Toward an Understanding of Intersectionality Methodology: A 30-Year Literature Synthesis of Black Women's Experiences in Higher Education," *Review of Educational Research* 90, no. 6 (2020): 751–87.

26. Richard Delgado and Jean Stefancic, *Critical Race Theory: An Introduction,* vol. 20 (New York: NYU Press, 2001).

27. Venus E. Evans-Winters, *Teaching Black Girls: Resiliency in Urban Classrooms* (New York: Peter Lang, 2005); Venus E. Evans-Winters and J. Esposito, "Other People's Daughters: Critical Race Feminism and Black Girls' Education," *Journal of Educational Foundations* 24, no. 1 (2010): 11–24; Joseph et al., "Black Female Adolescents and Racism in Schools: Experiences in a Colorblind Society"; S. Rowley, B. Kurtz-Costes, and S. M. Cooper, "The Schooling of African American Children," in *Handbook of Research on Schools, Schooling, and Human Development,* ed. J. L. Meece and J. S. Eccles (New York: Routledge, 2011), 275–92; US Census Bureau, "Quick Facts," https://www.census.gov/quickfacts/fact/table/US/LFE046219.

28. Quentin R. Alexander and Mary A. Hermann, "African-American Women's Experiences in Graduate Science, Technology, Engineering, and Mathematics Education at a Predominantly White University: A Qualitative Investigation," *Journal of Diversity in Higher Education* 9, no. 4 (2016): 307, doi:10.1037/a0003970; Maisie Gholson and Danny B. Martin, "Smart Girls, Black Girls, Mean Girls,

and Bullies: At the Intersection of Identities and the Mediating Role of Young Girls' Social Networks in Mathematical Communities of Practice," *Journal of Education* 194, no. 1 (2014): 19–33; Danny B. Martin, "Learning Mathematics While Black," *Journal of Educational Foundations* 26, no. 1 (2012): 47–66.

29. Joseph, "What Plato Took for Granted"; Walker, *Beyond Banneker*.

30. Joseph, "What Plato Took for Granted"; Ebony McGee, "Young, Black, Mathematically Gifted, and Stereotyped," *High School Journal* 96 (2013): 253–63; Walker, *Beyond Banneker*.

31. William F. Tate, "Critical Race Theory and Education: History, Theory, and Implications," *Review of Research in Education* 22 (1997): 195–247.

32. Danny B. Martin, *Mathematics Success and Failure among African American Youth: The Roles of Socio-Historical Context, Community Forces, School Influence, and Individual Agency* (Mahwah, NJ: Lawrence Erlbaum, 2000).

33. Daniel Solórzano and Dolores Delgado Bernal, "Critical Race Theory, Transformational Resistance and Social Justice: Chicana and Chicano Students in an Urban Context," *Urban Education* 36, no. 3 (2001): 308–42.

34. Paulo Freire, *Pedagogy of the Oppressed* (New York: Bloomsbury, 2000).

35. Cynthia B. Dillard, "The Substance of Things Hoped for, the Evidence of Things Not Seen: Examining an Endarkened Feminist Epistemology in Educational Research and Leadership," *International Journal of Qualitative Studies in Education* 13, no. 6 (2000): 661–81.

36. Terri Watson, Twitter, November 18, 2019.

37. Jae Hoon Lim, "The Road Not Taken: Two African-American Girls' Experiences with School Mathematics," *Race Ethnicity and Education* 11, no. 3 (2008): 303–17.

38. Tamara T. Butler, "Black Girl Cartography: Black Girlhood and Place-making in Education Research" *Review of Research in Education* 42, no. 1 (2018): 28–45.

39. Crenshaw, "Mapping the Margins"; Evans-Winters and Esposito, "Other People's Daughters."

40. Patricia Collins, "Intersections of Race, Class, Gender, and Nation. Some Implications for Black Family Studies," *Journal of Comparative Family Studies* 29 (1998): 27–34.

41. Joseph et al., "Black Girls' and Women's Persistence in the P–20 Mathematics Pipeline"; Nicole M. Joseph, Chayla M. Haynes, and Floyd Cobb, eds., *Interrogating Whiteness and Relinquishing Power: White Faculty's Commitment to Racial Consciousness in STEM Classrooms* (New York: Peter Lang, 2016); Danny B. Martin, "E (race) ing Race from a National Conversation on Mathematics Teaching and Learning: The National Mathematics Advisory Panel as White Institutional Space," *Montana Mathematics Enthusiast* 5 (2008): 387–98.

42. Ayshee Bhaduri, "Stacey Abrams: Lawyer, Voting Rights Activist who Turned Georgia Blue," *Hindustan Times*, January 6, 2021, https://www.hindustan times.com/world-news/stacey-abrams-lawyer-voting-rights-activist-who-turned -georgia-blue/story-VoL2UMCocn79Wx5KbtvWhP.html.

43. Sandra Harding, "Rethinking Standpoint Epistemology: What Is Strong Objectivity?," in *Feminist Epistemologies*, ed. Linda Alcoff and Elizabeth Potter (New York: Routledge, 1993).

44. Walter G. Secada, "Agenda Setting, Enlightened Self-Interest, and Equity in Mathematics Education," *Peabody Journal of Education* 66, no. 2 (1989): 22–56.

45. Secada, "Agenda Setting, Enlightened Self-Interest, and Equity."

CHAPTER 1

1. Lori D. Patton et al., "Why We Can't Wait:(Re) examining the Opportunities and Challenges for Black Women and Girls in Education (Guest Editorial)," *Journal of Negro Education* 85, no. 3 (2016): 194–98.

2. Maisie L. Gholson, "Clean Corners and Algebra: A Critical Examination of the Constructed Invisibility of Black Girls and Women in Mathematics," *Journal of Negro Education* 85, no. 3 (2016): 290–301; Sara N. Hottinger, *Inventing the Mathematician: Gender, Race, and Our Cultural Understanding of Mathematics* (New York: SUNY Press, 2016); Nicole M. Joseph, "What Plato Took for Granted: An Examination of the First Five African American Female Mathematicians and What That Says about Resistance to the Western Epistemological Canon," in *Women of Color in STEM: Navigating the Workforce*, ed. Julia Ballenger et al. (Charlotte, NC: Information Age Publishing, 2017), 3–38; Nicole M. Joseph, "The Invisibility of Black Girls in Mathematics," *Journal of Virginia Mathematics Teachers* 44, no. 1 (2017): 21–7.

3. Nicole M. Joseph and Donna Jordan-Taylor, "The Value of a Triangle: Mathematics Education in Industrial and Classical Schools in the Segregated South," *Journal of Negro Education* 85, no. 4 (2016): 444–61.

4. Farah Jasmine Griffin, "On Black Girlhood," Public Books, November 1, 2016, https://www.publicbooks.org/on-black-girlhood/#fn-7397-1, paragraph 7.

5. Kabria Baumgartner, "Searching for Sarah: Black Girlhood, Education, and the Archive," *History of Education Quarterly* 60, no. 1 (2020): 73–85.

6. Stephen Kendrick and Paul Kendrick, *Sarah's Long Walk: The Free Blacks of Boston and How Their Struggle for Equality Changed America*, vol. 150 (Boston: Beacon Press, 2004).

7. Elizabeth L. Ihle, *History of Black Women's Education in the South* (Washington, DC: US Department of Education, 1986).

8. Ihle, *History of Black Women's Education in the South.*

9. bell hooks, *Talking Back: Thinking Feminist, Thinking Black* (Boston: South End Press, 1989).

10. Heather Andrea Williams, *Self-Taught: African American Education in Slavery and Freedom* (Charlotte: University of North Carolina Press, 2009); James D. Anderson, *The Education of Blacks in the South, 1860–1935* (Charlotte: University of North Carolina Press, 1988).

11. Anderson, *Education of Blacks in the South, 1860–1935.*

12. Elizabeth L. Ihle, *Black Girls and Women in Elementary Education: History of Black Women's Education in the South, 1865–Present. Instructional Modules for Educators, Module I* (Washington, DC: US Department of Education, 1986), 3–4.

13. Ihle, *Black Women's Education in the South, Instructional Modules for Educators, Module 1.*

14. Ihle, *Black Women's Education in the South, Instructional Modules for Educators,* *Module 1*, 4.

15. Ihle, *Black Women's Education in the South, Instructional Modules for Educators,* *Module 1*, 4.

16. Ihle, *Black Women's Education in the South, Instructional Modules for Educators,* *Module 1*, 4.

17. Jacqueline Jones, *Labor of Love, Labor of Sorrow: Black Women, Work, and the Family, from Slavery to the Present* (New York: Basic Books, 2009).

18. Linda M. Perkins, "The Black Female American Missionary Association Teacher in the South, 1861–1870," in *Black Americans in North Carolina and the South,* ed. Jeffrey J. Crow and Flora J. Hatley (Charlotte: University of North Carolina Press, 1984), 122–36.

19. Perkins, "The Black Female American Missionary," 125.

20. Perkins, "The Black Female American Missionary," 126.

21. Perkins, "The Black Female American Missionary," 126.

22. Ihle, *Black Women's Education in the South, Instructional Modules for Educators,* *Module 1.*

23. Ihle, *Black Women's Education in the South, Instructional Modules for Educators,* *Module 1*, 3.

24. Ihle, *Black Women's Education in the South, Instructional Modules for Educators,* *Module 1*, 3.

25. Jacqueline Jones, *Labor of Love, Labor of Sorrow* (New York, Basic Books, 1985). This well-researched study will give the reader a greater appreciation for Black women's long tradition of work outside the home.

26. Ruth Miller Elson, *Guardians of Tradition: American Schoolbooks of the Nineteenth Century* (Lincoln: University of Nebraska Press, 1964), 1.

27. Elson, *Guardians of Tradition.*

28. Ihle, *Black Women's Education in the South, Instructional Modules for Educators,* *Module 1.*

29. William Biglow, *The Youths Library,* vol. I (Salem, MA: Joshua Cushing, 1803), 71.

30. Ihle, *Black Women's Education in the South, Instructional Modules for Educators,* *Module 1.*

31. Anderson, *Education of Blacks in the South, 1860–1935;* Joseph and Jordan-Taylor, "The Value of a Triangle."

32. Anderson, *Education of Blacks in the South, 1860–1935;* Ihle, *Black Women's Education in the South, Instructional Modules for Educators, Module II.*

33. Joseph and Jordan-Taylor, "The Value of a Triangle," 450.

34. Joseph and Jordan-Taylor, "The Value of a Triangle," 450.

35. Anderson, *Education of Blacks in the South, 1860–1935.*

36. Ihle, *Black Women's Education in the South, Instructional Modules for Educators,* *Module II.*

37. Combahee River Collective, "The Combahee River Collective Statement," *Home Girls: A Black Feminist Anthology* (1983): 264–74. This statement was created and made by a group of Black feminists whose main politic was working in the struggle against racial, sexual, heterosexual, and class oppression

through an integrated analysis given that the major systems of oppression are interlocking.

38. Combahee River Collective, "The Combahee River Collective Statement," 3.

39. Ihle, *Black Women's Education in the South, Instructional Modules for Educators, Module II*; Anderson, *Education of Blacks in the South, 1860–1935*.

40. Emilda B. Rivers, "Women, Minorities, and Persons with Disabilities in Science and Engineering," National Science Foundation, 2017.

41. Lawrence M. Clark, Toya J. Frank, and Julius Davis, "Conceptualizing the African American Mathematics Teacher as a Key Figure in the African American Education Historical Narrative," *Teachers College Record* 115, no. 2 (2013): 2.

42. Dan Battey and Luis A. Leyva, "A Framework for Understanding Whiteness in Mathematics Education," *Journal of Urban Mathematics Education* 9, no. 2 (2016): 49–80; Viveka Borum and Erica Walker, "What Makes the Difference? Black Women's Undergraduate and Graduate Experiences in Mathematics," *Journal of Negro Education* 81, no. 4 (2012): 366–78; Luis A. Leyva, "Black women's Counter-Stories of Resilience and Within-Group Tensions in the White, Patriarchal Space of Mathematics Education," *Journal for Research in Mathematics Education* 52, no. 2 (2021): 117–51.

43. Shannon Sullivan, *Revealing Whiteness: The Unconscious Habits of Racial Privilege* (Bloomington: Indiana University Press, 2006).

44. Roni Ellington, "Mathematics Teacher Education as a Racialized Experience," in *Interrogating Whiteness and Relinquishing Power: White Faculty's Commitment to Racial Consciousness in STEM Classrooms*, ed. Nicole M. Joseph et al. (New York: Peter Lange, 2016).

45. David L. Angus and Jeffrey E. Mirel, "Equality, Curriculum, and the Decline of the Academic Ideal: Detroit, 1930–1968," *History of Education Quarterly* 33, no. 2 (1993): 177–207; Joseph, "What Plato Took for Granted."

46. Jeannie Oakes, Rebecca Joseph, and Kate Muir, "Access and Achievement in Mathematics and Science: Inequalities That Endure and Change," in *Handbook of Research on Multicultural Education*, 2nd ed., ed. James A. Banks and Cherry A. McGee Banks (San Francisco: Jossey-Bass, 2004).

47. Oakes et al., "Access and Achievement in Mathematics and Science." See Daniel v. California, No. BC 214156.

48. Oakes et al., "Access and Achievement in Mathematics and Science."

49. Carter G. Woodson, *The Mis-Education of the Negro* (CreateSpace Independent Publishing Platform, 2010; first published 1933), 65.

50. Woodson, *The Mis-Education of the Negro*, 78.

51. Danny B. Martin, *Mathematics Success and Failure Among African-American Youth: The Roles of Sociohistorical Context, Community Forces, School Influence, and Individual Agency* (New York: Routledge, 2000).

52. Martin, *Mathematics Success and Failure Among African-American Youth*, 37.

53. Borum and Walker, "What Makes the Difference?"; Abbe H. Herzig, "Becoming Mathematicians: Women and Students of Color Choosing and Leaving Doctoral Mathematics," *Review of Educational Research* 74, no. 2 (2004): 171–214.

54. Borum and Walker, "What Makes the Difference?"

55. Borum and Walker, "What Makes the Difference?"

56. Borum and Walker, "What Makes the Difference?," 373.

57. *Mathematically Gifted and Black*, retrieved from https://mathematicallygifted andblack.com/.

58. Nicole M. Joseph, Kara Mitchell Viesca, and Margarita Bianco, "Black Female Adolescents and Racism in Schools: Experiences in a Colorblind Society," *High School Journal* 100, no. 1 (2016): 4–25.

59. Chimamanda Ngozi Adichie, "The Danger of a Single Story," TEDGlobal, 2009, https://www.ted.com/talks/chimamanda_ngozi_adichie_the_danger _of_a_single_story.

60. Rose M. Pringle et al., "Factors Influencing Elementary Teachers' Positioning of African American Girls as Science and Mathematics Learners," *School Science and Mathematics* 112, no. 4 (2012): 217–29.

61. Stephanie Jones, "Identities of Race, Class, and Gender Inside and Outside the Math Classroom: A Girls' Math Club as a Hybrid Possibility," *Feminist Teacher* (2003): 220–33.

62. Jones, "Identities of Race, Class, and Gender Inside and Outside the Math Classroom," 225.

63. Nicole M. Joseph, Samantha S. Marshall, and Mariah Harmon, "NSF Funding and Broadening Participation: Examining and Problematizing a Case of Black Women in Mathematics" (paper under review).

CHAPTER 2

1. David K. Cohen, *Teaching and its Predicaments* (Cambridge, MA: Harvard University Press, 2011).

2. Anne C. Frenzel, Reinhard Pekrun, and Thomas Goetz, "Perceived Learning Environment and Students' Emotional Experiences: A Multilevel Analysis of Mathematics Classrooms," *Learning and Instruction* 17, no. 5 (2007): 478–93.

3. Barry J. Fraser, *Individualized Classroom Environment Questionnaire* (Melbourne: Australian Council for Educational Research, 2009); Campbell J. McRobbie and Barry J. Fraser, "Associations Between Student Outcomes and Psychosocial Science Environment," *Journal of Educational Research* 87, no. 2 (1993): 78–85; Eric M. Anderman et al., "Learning to Value Mathematics and Reading: Relations to Mastery and Performance-Oriented Instructional Practices," *Contemporary Educational Psychology* 26, no. 1 (2001): 76–95.

4. Frenzel et al., "Perceived Learning Environment and Students' Emotional Experiences."

5. Nicole M. Joseph, Meseret F. Hailu, and Jamaal Sharif Matthews, "Normalizing Black Girls' Humanity in Mathematics Classrooms," *Harvard Educational Review* 89, no. 1 (2019): 132–55.

6. Dan Battey and Luis A. Leyva, "A Framework for Understanding Whiteness in Mathematics Education," *Journal of Urban Mathematics Education* 9, no. 2 (2016): 49–80.

7. Tema Okun, "White Supremacy Culture," in *Dismantling Racism: A Workbook for Social Change Groups* (Durham, NC: Change Work, 2000).

8. Ilana S. Horn, *Motivated: Designing Math Classrooms Where Students Want to Join In* (Portsmouth, NH: Heinemann, 2017); Francis E. Su, "Mathematics for Human Flourishing," *American Mathematical Monthly* 124, no. 6 (2017): 483–93; Nicole M. Joseph and Norman Alston, "I Fear No Number: Black Girls' Experiences in eMode Learning Math Academy," in *Rehumanizing Mathematics for Black, Indigenous, and Latinx Students*, eds. Imani Goffney, Rochelle Gutierrez, and Melissa Boston (Reston, VA: NCTM, 2018), 51–62.

9. EdReports.org is an independent nonprofit designed to improve K–12 education. EdReports.org increases the capacity of teachers, administrators, and leaders to seek, identify, and demand the highest-quality instructional materials. Drawing upon expert educators, our reviews of instructional materials and support of smart adoption processes equip teachers with excellent materials nationwide. They are funded by the Gates Foundation, Carnegie Corporation of NY, and several other high-profile foundations.

10. "Dismantling Racism 2016 Workbook," dRworks, https://resourcegeneration .org/wp-content/uploads/2018/01/2016-dRworks-workbook.pdf.

11. Luis A. Leyva, "Black Women's Counter-Stories of Resilience and Within-Group Tensions in the White, Patriarchal Space of Mathematics Education," *Journal for Research in Mathematics Education* 52, no. 2 (2021).

12. Leyva, "Black Women's Counter-Stories of Resilience."

13. Sara N. Hottinger, *Inventing the Mathematician: Gender, Race, And Our Cultural Understanding of Mathematics* (Albany: SUNY Press, 2016); Danny B. Martin, "Race, Racial Projects, and Mathematics Education," *Journal for Research in Mathematics Education* 44, no. 1 (2013): 316–33; Taylor R. McNeill, Luis A. Leyva, and Brittany L. Marshall, "'They're Just Students. There's No Clear Distinction': The Operationalization of Colorblind, Gender-Neutral Instructor Discourses in Undergraduate Precalculus and Calculus" (under review).

14. Nicole M Joseph, Meseret Hailu, and Denise Boston, "Black Women's and Girls' Persistence in the P–20 Mathematics Pipeline: Two Decades of Children, Youth, and Adult Education Research," *Review of Research in Education* 41, no. 1 (2017): 203–27.

15. Floyd Cobb and Nicole M. Russell, "Meritocracy or Complexity: Problematizing Racial Disparities in Mathematics Assessment Within the Context of Curricular Structures, Practices, and Discourse," *Journal of Education Policy* 30, no. 5 (2015): 631–49.

16. Jae Hoon Lim, "The Road Not Taken: Two African-American Girls' Experiences with School Mathematics," *Race Ethnicity and Education* 11, no. 3 (2008): 303–17.

17. Lim, "The Road Not Taken," 310.

18. Lim, "The Road Not Taken," 309.

19. Shanyce L. Campbell, "For Colored Girls? Factors That Influence Teacher Recommendations into Advanced Courses for Black Girls," *Review of Black Political Economy* 39, no. 4 (2012): 389–402.

20. Campbell, "For Colored Girls?"
21. Maggie McBride, "The Theme of Individualism in Mathematics Education: An Examination of Mathematics Textbooks," *For the Learning of Mathematics* 14, no. 3 (1994): 36–42.
22. McBride, "The Theme of Individualism."
23. McBride, "The Theme of Individualism."
24. Robert Q. Berry III, "Mathematics Standards, Cultural Styles, and Learning Preferences: The Plight and the Promise of African American Students," *Clearing House* 76, no. 5 (2003): 244–49.
25. Joseph et al., "Normalizing Black Girls' Humanity."
26. Viveka Borum and Erica Walker, "What Makes the Difference? Black Women's Undergraduate and Graduate Experiences in Mathematics," *Journal of Negro Education* 81, no. 4 (2012): 366–78.
27. Luis A. Leyva, "Black Women's Counter-Stories of Resilience and Within-Group Tensions in the White, Patriarchal Space of Mathematics Education," *Journal for Research in Mathematics Education* 52, no. 2 (2021): 117-51.
28. Leyva, "Black Women's Counter-Stories," 34.
29. Irving Howe, "The Value of the Canon," *New Republic* 204, no. 7 (1991): 40–6.
30. Sandra Harding, *Whose Science? Whose Knowledge? Thinking From Women's Lives* (Ithaca, NY: Cornell University Press, 1991).
31. "Dismantling Racism 2016 Workbook," dRworks, https://resourcegeneration .org/wp-content/uploads/2018/01/2016-dRworks-workbook.pdf.
32. Sandra Harding, "'Strong Objectivity': A Response to the New Objectivity Question," *Synthese* 104, no. 3 (1995): 331.
33. Harding, "'Strong Objectivity,'" 331–49.
34. Common Core State Initiatives, "Standards for Mathematical Practice," http:// www.corestandards.org/Math/Practice/.
35. Joseph et al., "Normalizing Black Girls' Humanity."
36. Ilana Horn and Nicole M. Joseph, "Let Them Laugh: Using Humor in Math Class," *Teaching Math Culture*, https://teachingmathculture.wordpress.com /2019/08/21/let-them-laugh-using-humor-in-math-class/.
37. Julie Kern Schwerdtfeger and Angela Chan, "Counting Collections," *Teaching Children Mathematics* 13, no. 7 (2007): 356–61.
38. Paulo Freire, *Pedagogy of the Oppressed* (New York: Bloomsbury, 2018).
39. Joseph et al., "Normalizing Black Girls' Humanity."
40. Luis A. Leyva et al., "'It Seems Like They Purposefully Try to Make as Many Kids Drop': An Analysis of Logics and Mechanisms of Racial-Gendered Inequality in Introductory Mathematics Instruction," *Journal of Higher Education* (in press).
41. Horn, *Motivated*; Joseph, and Alston, "I Fear No Number"; Su, *Mathematics for Human Flourishing*.
42. Joseph and Alston, "I Fear No Number."
43. Joseph and Alston, "I Fear No Number," 554.
44. Aria S. Halliday, *The Black Girlhood Studies Collection* (Toronto: Women's Press, 2019).

45. Ilana S. Horn, "Accountable Argumentation as a Participant Structure to Support Learning Through Disagreement" (presented at the annual meeting of the American Educational Research Association, Montréal, Quebec, Canada, April 1999); Courtney B. Cazden, *Classroom Discourse: The Language of Teaching and Learning* (Portsmouth, NH: Heinemann, 1988).
46. Horn, *Motivated*, 8.
47. Sara Jones, "Measuring Reading Motivation: A Cautionary Tale," *Reading Teacher* 74, no. 1 (2020): 79–89.
48. Horn, *Motivated*.
49. Horn, *Motivated*, 8.
50. Horn, *Motivated*, 9.
51. Su, "Mathematics for Human Flourishing."
52. Joseph et al., "Normalizing Black Girls' Humanity."
53. Joseph et al., "Normalizing Black Girls' Humanity," 149.
54. Su, *Mathematics for Human Flourishing*, 486.
55. Jakita O. Thomas, "The Computational Algorithmic Thinking (CAT) Capability Flow: An Approach to Articulating CAT Capabilities Over Time in African-American Middle-school Girls," in *Proceedings of the 49th ACM Technical Symposium on Computer Science Education*, 149–54 (New York: Association for Computing Machinery, 2018).
56. Jakita O. Thomas et al., "Exploring the difficulties African American middle school girls face enacting computational algorithmic thinking over three years while designing games for social change," *Computer Supported Cooperative Work (CSCW)* 26, no. 4 (2017): 389–421.
57. Personal Communication with Dr. Jakita Thomas.
58. Nicole M. Joseph, "Black Feminist Mathematics Pedagogies (Black FMP): A Curricular Confrontation to Gendered Antiblackness in the US Mathematics Education System, *Curriculum Inquiry* (in press).
59. Joseph, "Black Feminist Mathematics Pedagogies (Black FMP).
60. Taylor R. McNeill, Luis A. Leyva, and Brittany L. Marshall, "'They're Just Students. There's No Clear Distinction': The Operationalization of Colorblind, Gender-Neutral Instructor Discourses in Undergraduate Precalculus and Calculus" (under review).
61. Dania V. Francis, "Sugar and Spice and Everything Nice? Teacher Perceptions of Black Girls in the Classroom," *Review of Black Political Economy* 39, no. 3 (2012): 311–20.
62. Su, *Mathematics for Human Flourishing*, 490.

CHAPTER 3

1. William H. Schmidt, Hsing Chi Wang, and Curtis C. McKnight, "Curriculum Coherence: An Examination of US Mathematics and Science Content Standards from an International Perspective," *Journal of Curriculum Studies* 37, no. 5 (2005): 525–59.

2. National Research Council, *On Evaluating Curricular Effectiveness: Judging the Quality of K–12 Mathematics Evaluations* (Washington, DC: National Academies Press, 2004).

3. Elizabeth A. Davis and Joseph S. Krajcik, "Designing Educative Curriculum Materials to Promote Teacher Learning," *Educational Researcher* 34, no. 3 (2005): 3–14; Mary Kay Stein, Janine Remillard, and Margaret S. Smith, "How Curriculum Influences Student Learning," in *Second Handbook of Research on Mathematics Teaching and Learning*, ed. Frank Lester Jr. (Charlotte, NC: Information Age Publishing, 2007), 319–70; Pam Grossman and Clarissa Thompson, "Learning from Curriculum Materials: Scaffolds for New Teachers?" *Teaching and Teacher Education* 24, no. 8 (2008): 2014–26.

4. Caroline Ebby et al., "Community Based Mathematics Project: Conceptualizing Access through Locally Relevant Mathematics Curricula," *Penn GSE Perspectives on Urban Education* 8, no. 2 (2011): 11–18.

5. Alan H. Schoenfeld, "The Math Wars," *Educational Policy* 18, no. 1 (2004): 253–86.

6. Janine T. Remillard, Barbara Harris, and Roberto Agodini, "The Influence of Curriculum Material Design on Opportunities for Student Learning," *ZDM* 46, no. 5 (2014): 735–49.

7. Marjorie Henningsen and Mary Kay Stein, "Mathematical Tasks and Student Cognition: Classroom-Based Factors that Support and Inhibit High-Level Mathematical Thinking and Reasoning," *Journal for Research in Mathematics Education* 28, no. 5 (1997): 524–49.

8. Nicole M. Joseph, Ashli-Ann Douglass, and Mariah Harmon, "'I Like to do More Hands-On Stuff than Just Worksheets,' High School Black Girls' Stories of their Experiences in Urban Mathematics Classrooms," under review.

9. Keonya C. Booker and Jae Hoon Lim, "Belongingness and Pedagogy: Engaging African American Girls in Middle School Mathematics," *Youth & Society* 50, no. 8 (2018): 1037–55.

10. Booker and Lim, "Belongingness and Pedagogy: Engaging African American Girls in Middle School Mathematics," 1046.

11. Booker and Lim, "Belongingness and Pedagogy: Engaging African American Girls in Middle School Mathematics," 1046.

12. Margaret Schwan Smith and Mary Kay Stein, "Reflections on Practice: Selecting and Creating Mathematical Tasks: From Research to Practice," *Mathematics Teaching in the Middle School* 3, no. 5 (1998): 344–50.

13. Magdalene Lampert et al., "Using Designed Instructional Activities to Enable Novices to Manage Ambitious Mathematics Teaching," in *Instructional Explanations in the Disciplines* (Boston: Springer, 2010), 129–41.

14. Jo Boaler, Cathey Williams, and Amanda Confer, "Fluency Without Fear: Research Evidence on the Best Ways to Learn Math Facts," YouCubed at Stanford University, January 28, 2015, https://www.youcubed.org/wp-content/uploads/2017/09/Fluency-Without-Fear-1.28.15.pdf.

15. Clifton B. Parker, "Research Shows the Best Ways to Learn Math," Stanford Graduate School of Education, January 29, 2015, https://ed.stanford.edu/news/learning-math-without-fear.

16. Common Core State Standards Initiative, "Standards for Mathematical Practice," http://www.corestandards.org/Math/Practice/; National Research Council and Mathematics Learning Study Committee, *Adding It Up: Helping Children Learn Mathematics* (Washington, DC: National Academies Press, 2001).

17. Nicole M. Joseph and Norman Alston, "I Fear No Number: Black Girls' Experiences in eMode Learning Math Academy," in *Rehumanizing Mathematics for Black, Indigenous, and Latinx Students*, eds. Imani Goffney, Rochelle Gutierrez, and Melissa Boston (Reston, VA: NCTM, 2018), 51–62.

18. Megan L. Franke, Elham Kazemi, and Daniel Battey, "Mathematics Teaching and Classroom Practice," in *Second Handbook of Research on Mathematics Teaching and Learning*, ed. Frank Lester Jr. (Charlotte, NC: Information Age Publishing, 2007), 225–56.

19. Paulo Freire, *Pedagogy of the Oppressed* (New York: Bloomsbury, 2018).

20. Nicole M. Joseph, Meseret Hailu, and Denise Boston, "Black Women's and Girls' Persistence in the P–20 Mathematics Pipeline: Two Decades of Children, Youth, and Adult Education Research," *Review of Research in Education* 41, no. 1 (2017): 203–27.

21. Stein et al., "How Curriculum Influences Student Learning"

22. Janine T. Remillard and Luke Reinke, "Complicating Scripted Curriculum: Can Scripts Be Educative for Teachers" (paper presented at the annual meeting of the American Educational Research Association, Vancouver, British Columbia, 2012).

23. Robyn Zevenbergen, "'Cracking the Code' of Mathematics Classrooms: School Success as a Function of Linguistic, Social, and Cultural Background," in *Multiple Perspectives on Mathematics Teaching and Learning*, ed. Jo Boaler (Westport, CT: Praeger, 2000), 201–223.

24. June Mark et al., "How Do Districts Choose Mathematics Textbooks," in *Mathematics Curriculum: Issues, Trends, and Future Direction* (Reston, VA: National Council of Teachers of Mathematics, 2010), 199–211.

25. Mark et al., "How Do Districts Choose Mathematics Textbooks," 208.

26. Mark et al., "How Do Districts Choose Mathematics Textbooks," 206–209.

27. National Center for Education Statistics, "Digest of Education Statistics," https://nces.ed.gov/programs/digest/d17/tables/dt17_209.10.asp?current=yes.

28. Richard M. Ingersol et al., "Seven Trends: The Transformation of the Teaching Force," CPRE Research Report# RR 2018-2, University of Pennsylvania Consortium for Policy Research in Education, updated October 2018.

29. *Othermothering* is a word coined by CRT scholar Adrian Dixon to describe teachers and professors who serve as proxy moms for many students. Travis J. Bristol and Ramon B. Goings, "Exploring the Boundary-Heightening Experiences of Black Male Teachers: Lessons for Teacher Education Programs," *Journal of Teacher Education* 70, no. 1 (2019): 51–64; Travis J. Bristol and Marcelle Mentor, "Policing and Teaching: The Positioning of Black Male Teachers as Agents in the Universal Carceral Apparatus," *Urban Review* 50, no. 2 (2018): 218–34; Goli M. Rezai-Rashti and Wayne J. Martino, "Black Male Teachers as Role Models: Resisting the Homogenizing Impulse of Gender and Racial

Affiliation," *American Educational Research Journal* 47, no. 1 (2010): 37–64; Adrienne Dixson and Jeannine E. Dingus, "In Search of Our Mothers' Gardens: Black Women Teachers and Professional Socialization," *Teachers College Record* 110, no. 4 (2008): 805–37.

30. Mark et al., "How Do Districts Choose Mathematics Textbooks."

31. James Hiebert and James W. Stigler, "Teaching Versus Teachers as a Lever for Change: Comparing a Japanese and a US Perspective on Improving Instruction," *Educational Researcher* 46, no. 4 (2017): 169–76.

32. Susan J. Lamon, *Teaching Fractions and Ratios for Understanding: Essential Content Knowledge and Instructional Strategies for Teachers* (New York: Routledge, 2020), 25.

33. Janine T. Remillard, "Curriculum Materials in Mathematics Education Reform: A Framework for Examining Teachers' Curriculum Development," *Curriculum Inquiry* 29, no. 3 (1999): 315–42.

34. Seymour Bernard Sarason, *The Culture of the School and the Problem of Change* (Boston: Allyn and Bacon, 1982).

35. Susan Stodolsky, "Is Teaching Really by the Book?" *Teachers College Record* 100, no. 6 (1999): 159–84.

36. Janine Remillard, "Mapping the relationship between written and enacted curriculum: Examining teachers' decision making," in *Invited Lectures from the 13th International Congress on Mathematical Education* (Edinburgh: Springer, Cham, 2018), 483–500.

37. Charles Munter and Cara Haines, "Mathematics Teachers' Enactment of Cognitively Demanding Tasks and Students' Perception of Racial Differences in Opportunity," *Mathematical Thinking and Learning* 21, no. 3 (2019): 155–77.

38. Munter and Haines, "Mathematics Teachers' Enactment of Cognitively Demanding Tasks," 155–77.

39. Mark et al., "How Do Districts Choose Mathematics Textbooks."

40. Robert E. Reys, "Curricular Controversy in the Math Wars: A Battle Without Winners," *Phi Delta Kappan* 83, no. 3 (2001): 255–58.

41. Mary Elizabeth Williams, "New York Schools Assigns Racist Word-Problems to Fourth-Graders," *Salon,* February 22, 2013, https://www.salon.com/2013 /02/22/new_york_school_assigns_racist_word_problems_to_fourth_graders/.

42. Ron Dicker, "Slave-Related Math Questions for 4th-Graders Spark Outrage at P.S. 59 in New York," *Huffpost,* February 22, 2013, https://www.huffpost.com /entry/slave-math-question_n_2740909?utm_hp_ref=new-york&ir=New +York.

43. "Georgia Parents Upset Over New Case of Math Homework Referencing Slavery," *Fox News,* November 20, 2014, https://www.foxnews.com/us/georgia -parents-upset-over-new-case-of-math-homework-referencing-slavery.

44. Valerie Strauss, "Slaves Used As Part of 3rd Grade Math Questions," *Washington Post,* January 8, 2012, https://www.washingtonpost.com/blogs/answer -sheet/post/slaves-used-as-part-of-3rd-grade-math-questions/2012/01/08 /gIQA9P8NkP_blog.html.

45. Lauren Effron, "Georgia School Investigates Slave Math Problems," *ABC News*, January 10, 2012, https://abcnews.go.com/blogs/headlines/2012/01/georgia-school-investigates-slave-math-problems.

46. Effron, "Georgia School Investigates Slave Math Problems."

47. "Black 2nd-Graders at L. A. Elementary School Get Math Homework with a Word Problem About Slavery," *The Root* via *History News Network*, February 14, 2017, https://historynewsnetwork.org/article/165195.

48. Margaret Hartmann, "NYC Teachers Give Fourth-Graders Math Problems About Dead Slaves, Whippings," *New York Intelligencer*, February 21, 2013, https://nymag.com/intelligencer/2013/02/nyc-kids-get-math-worksheet-on-slaves-whippings.html.

49. Ebony O. McGee and Andrew L. Hostetler, "Historicizing Mathematics and Mathematizing Social Studies for Social Justice: A Call for Integration," *Equity & Excellence in Education* 47, no. 2 (2014): 208–29.

50. Freire, *Pedagogy of the Oppressed*.

51. Jane Yamamoto, "Investigation into Black History Month Homework Assignment That Left Parents Outraged," San Diego News Channel 7, February 12, 2017, https://www.nbcsandiego.com/news/national-international/lausd-racial-undertones-math-homework-black-history-month/2033490/.

52. Barbara Omolade, "A Black Feminist Pedagogy," *Women's Studies Quarterly* 15, no. 3/4 (1987): 32–9.

53. Langston Hughes, *The Dream Keeper and Other Poems* (New York: Knopf Books for Young Readers, 1996).

54. Tiffany M. Nyachae, "Complicated Contradictions Amid Black Feminism and Millennial Black Women Teachers Creating Curriculum for Black Girls," *Gender and Education* 28, no. 6 (2016): 786–806.

55. Nyachae, "Complicated Contradictions Amid Black Feminism," 786–806.

56. Nyachae, "Complicated Contradictions Amid Black Feminism," 786–806.

CHAPTER 4

1. Ruth Nicole Brown, *Hear Our Truths: The Creative Potential of Black Girlhood* (Champaign: University of Illinois Press, 2013), 1.

2. Brown, *Hear Our Truths*, 1.

3. bell hooks, "The oppositional gaze: Black female spectators," in *The Feminism and Visual Culture Reader*, ed. Amelia Jones (New York: Routledge: 2003), 94–105.

4. Danny B. Martin, "Beyond Missionaries or Cannibals: Who Should Teach Mathematics to African American Children?," *High School Journal* 91, no. 1 (2007): 6–28.

5. Gholdy Muhammad, *Cultivating Genius: An Equity Framework for Culturally and Historically Responsive Literacy* (New York: Scholastic, 2020), 10.

6. Chayla M. Haynes et al., "Toward an Understanding of Intersectionality Methodology: A 30–Year Literature Synthesis of Black Women's Experiences in Higher Education," *Review of Educational Research* 90, no. 6 (2020): 751–87.

7. Shelah Marie Jefferson-Isaac, "They Count Also: The Experiences of African American Girls in Elementary School with Mathematics" (PhD dissertation, Hofstra University, 2006), 50, 71.

8. Jefferson-Isaac, "They Count Also," 73.

9. Nicole M. Joseph and Norman V. Alston, "I Fear No Number: Black Girls' Experiences In eMode Learning Math Academy," in *Rehumanizing Mathematics for Black, Indigenous, and Latinx Students*, ed. Imani Goffney et al. (Reston, VA: NCTM, 2018), 58.

10. Cirecie West-Olatunji et al., "How African American Middle School Girls Position Themselves as Mathematics and Science Learners," *International Journal of Learning* 14, no. 9 (2008), 223.

11. Nicole M. Joseph, Meseret Hailu, and Jamaal Matthews, "Normalizing Black Girls' Humanities in Mathematics Classrooms," *Harvard Education Review* 89, no.1 (2019): 144.

12. Keonya C. Booker and Jae Hoon Lim. "Belongingness and Pedagogy: Engaging African American Girls in Middle School Mathematics," *Youth & Society* 50, no. 8 (2018): 1045.

13. Booker and Lim, "Belongingness and Pedagogy," 1037–1055.

14. Tamra C. Ragland, "Don't Count Me Out: A Feminist Study of African American Girls' Experiences in Mathematics" (PhD dissertation, University of Cincinnati, 2012).

15. Ragland, "Don't Count Me Out," 75.

16. Booker and Lim, "Belongingness and Pedagogy," 1044.

17. Franita Ware, "Warm Demander Pedagogy: Culturally Responsive Teaching that Supports a Culture of Achievement for African American Students," *Urban Education* 41, no. 4 (2006): 427–45; Judith Kleinfeld, "Effective teachers of Eskimo and Indian students," *School Review* 83, no. 2 (1975): 301–44.

18. Shelah Marie Jefferson-Isaac, "They Count Also: The Experiences of African American Girls in Elementary School with Mathematics" (PhD dissertation, Hofstra University, 2006), 72.

19. Jefferson-Isaac, "They Count Also," 73.

20. Nicole M. Joseph, Ashli-Ann Douglas, and Mariah Harmon, "'I Like to do More Hands-On Stuff than Just Worksheets': High School Black Girls' Stories of their Experiences in Urban Mathematics Classrooms" (under review).

21. Joseph et al., "'I Like to do More Hands-On Stuff than Just Worksheets.'"

22. Booker and Lim, "Belongingness and Pedagogy,"1046.

23. Jefferson-Isaac, "They Count Also," 74.

24. Sueanne E. McKinney et al., "An examination of the instructional practices of mathematics teachers in urban schools," *Preventing School Failure: Alternative Education for Children and Youth* 53, no. 4 (2009): 278–84.

25. Nicole M. Joseph and Bethany Rittle-Johnson, "Black Girls' Perspectives of Instructional Strategies in Urban Middle-School Mathematics Classrooms" (paper presented for the American Education Research Association, 2020).

26. Joseph and Rittle-Johnson, "Black Girls' Perspectives of Instructional Strategies."

27. Ragland, "Don't Count Me Out," 85.

28. Joseph et al., "'I Like to do More Hands-On Stuff than Just Worksheets.'"
29. Joseph et al., "'I Like to do More Hands-On Stuff than Just Worksheets.'"
30. Joseph et al., "'I Like to do More Hands-On Stuff than Just Worksheets.'"
31. Dorinda J. Carter Andrews et al., "The Impossibility of Being 'Perfect and White': Black Girls' Racialized and Gendered Schooling Experiences," *American Educational Research Journal* 56, no. 6 (2019): 2531–72.
32. Joseph et al., "'I Like to do More Hands-On Stuff than Just Worksheets.'"
33. Joseph and Alston, "I Fear No Number," 58.
34. Booker and Lim, "Belongingness and pedagogy," 1047.
35. bell hooks, "Sisterhood: Political Solidarity Between Women," *Feminist Review* 23, no. 1 (1986): 125–38.
36. Danny B. Martin, Paula Price, and Roxanne Moore, "Refusing Systemic Violence Against Black Children: Toward a Black Liberatory Mathematics Education," in *Critical Race Theory in Mathematics Education,* eds. Julius Davis and Christopher Jett (New York: Routledge, 2019).
37. Nicole M. Joseph, "Black Feminist Mathematics Pedagogies (BlackFMP): A Curricular Confrontation to Gendered Antiblackness in the US Mathematics Education System," *Curriculum Inquiry* 51, no. 1 (2021): 75–97.
38. Carl A. Grant, "Radical Hope, Education and Humility," in *The Future Is Black: Afropessimism, Fugitivity, and Radical Hope in Education,* eds. Carl A. Grant, Ashley N. Woodson, and Michael J. Dumans (New York: Routledge, 2020), 65–68.
39. Grant, "Radical Hope, Education and Humility," 66.
40. Stephanie Jones, "Identities of Race, Class, and Gender Inside and Outside the Math Classroom: A Girls' Math Club as a Hybrid Possibility," *Feminist Teacher* (2003), 220–33.
41. Rebecca Epstein, Jamilia Blake, and Thalia González, "Girlhood Interrupted: The Erasure of Black Girls' Childhood," Georgetown Law Center, Center on Poverty and Inequality, June 27, 2027.
42. Joseph et al., "'I Like to do More Hands-On Stuff than Just Worksheets.'"
43. Ebony O. McGee, "Robust and fragile mathematical identities: A framework for exploring racialized experiences and high achievement among black college students," *Journal for Research in Mathematics Education* 46, no. 5 (2015): 599–625.
44. bell hooks, *Teaching to Transgress* (New York: Routledge 2014), 12.
45. Megan L. Franke, Elham Kazemi, and Daniel Battey, "Mathematics Teaching and Classroom Practice," in *Second Handbook of Research on Mathematics Teaching and Learning,* ed. Frank Lester Jr. (Charlotte, NC: Information Age Publishing, 2007), 225–56.
46. Office of Civil Rights, STEM Course Taking, 2018, https://www2.ed.gov/about/offices/list/ocr/docs/stem-course-taking.pdf.
47. Phillip B. Levine and David J. Zimmerman, "The benefit of additional high-school math and science classes for young men and women," *Journal of Business & Economic Statistics* 13, no. 2 (1995), 137–49.
48. Ilana S. Horn, *Motivated: Designing Math Classrooms Where Students Want to Join in* (Portsmouth, NH: Heinemann, 2017).

CHAPTER 5

1. Rann Miller, "The Anti-Black Intellectual Hierarchy Built By Standardized Testing Needs To Come Down," *RaceBaitr,* January 21, 2020, https://racebaitr .com/2020/01/21/the-anti-black-intellectual-hierarchy-built-by-standardized -testing-needs-to-come-down/.

2. John Rosales and Tim Walker, "The Racists Beginnings of Standardized Testing," National Education Association, March 20, 2021, https://www.nea.org /advocating-for-change/new-from-nea/racist-beginnings-standardized-testing.

3. Jodi S. Cohen, "A Teenager Didn't Do Her Online Schoolwork. So a Judge Sent Her to Juvenile Detention," *ProPublica,* July 14, 2020, https://www.propublica .org/article/a-teenager-didnt-do-her-online-schoolwork-so-a-judge-sent-her-to -juvenile-detention.

4. Anya Kamenetz, "States Must Test Student Learning This Year, Biden Administration Says," National Public Radio, February 23, 2021, https://www.npr.org /sections/coronavirus-live-updates/2021/02/23/970520559/states-must-test -student-learning-this-spring-biden-administration-says.

5. "Development Process," Common Core State Standards Initiative, http://www .corestandards.org/about-the-standards/development-process/.

6. Nicole M. Joseph and Floyd Cobb, "Antiblackness is in the Air: Problematizing Black Students' Mathematics Education Pathways from Curriculum to Standardized Assessment," in *Critical Race Theory in Mathematics Education,* ed. Julius Davis et al. (New York: Routledge, 2019).

7. J. Michael Shaughnessy, "NCTM Action on the Common Core Standards for Mathematics," National Council of Teachers of Mathematics, November 2010, https://www.nctm.org/News-and-Calendar/Messages-from-the-President /Archive/J_-Michael-Shaughnessy/NCTM,-Action-on-the-Common-Core -State-Standards-for-Mathematics/#:ffi:text=The%20first%20NCTM%20 task%20force,major%20curriculum%20and%20standards%20publications.

8. Shaughnessy, "NCTM Action on the Common Core Standards."

9. "Standards for Mathematical Practice," Common Core State Standards Initiative, http://www.corestandards.org/Math/Practice/.

10. "Standards for Mathematical Practice," Common Core State Standards Initiative.

11. "Standards for Mathematical Practice," Common Core State Standards Initiative.

12. "Fourth Grade NAEP Mathematics Scores," National Center for Education Statistics, https://www.nationsreportcard.gov/mathematics/states/groups /?grade=8.

13. "Total Black Girls Enrolled in K-12 by State," National Center for Education Statistics, http://nces.ed.gov/ccd/elsi/; "Fourth Grade NAEP Mathematics Scores," National Center for Education Statistics, https://www.nations reportcard.gov/mathematics/states/groups/?grade=8.

14. "About NAEP: A Common Measure of Student Achievement," National Center for Education Statistics, https://nces.ed.gov/nationsreportcard/about/.

15. Danny B. Martin, "Hidden Assumptions and Unaddressed Questions in Mathematics for all Rhetoric," *Mathematics Educator* 13, no. 2 (2003); Danny B. Martin, "The Collective Black and Principles to Actions," *Journal of Urban Mathematics Education* 8, no. 1 (2015).

16. Melissa Clinedinst and Pooja Patel, "2018 State of College Admission," National Association for College Admission Counseling (2018): 4.

17. Nicole M. Joseph, Meseret Hailu, and Denise Boston, "Black Women's and Girls' Persistence in the P–20 Mathematics Pipeline: Two Decades of Children, Youth, and Adult Education Research," *Review of Research in Education* 41, no. 1 (2017): 203–27.

18. Samantha Lindsay, "What's the Average High School GPA?," *PrepScholar*, January 19, 2020, https://blog.prepscholar.com/whats-the-average-high-school-gpa.

19. Lindsay, "What's the Average High School GPA?"

20. Margaret Zamudio et al., *Critical Race Theory Matters: Education and Ideology* (New York: Routledge, 2011).

21. Zamudio et al., *Critical Race Theory Matters: Education and Ideology*, 12.

22. Joseph and Cobb, "Antiblackness is in the Air"; William Schmidt and Curtis McKnight, *Inequality for All: The Challenge of Unequal Opportunity in American Schools* (New York: Teachers College Press, 2015).

23. Floyd Cobb and Nicole M. Russell, "Meritocracy or Complexity: Problematizing Racial Disparities in Mathematics Assessment within the Context of Curricular Structures, Practices, and Discourse," *Journal of Education Policy* 30, no. 5 (2015), 631–49.

24. Cobb and Russell, "Meritocracy or Complexity."

25. Linda Darling-Hammond, *The Flat World and Education: How America's Commitment to Equity Will Determine Our Future* (New York: Teachers College Press, 2015); Teresa K. Dunleavy, "Delegating Mathematical Authority as a Means to Strive Toward Equity," *Journal of Urban Mathematics Education* 8, no. 1 (2015); Sean Kelly, "The Black-White Gap in Mathematics Course Taking," *Sociology of Education* 82, no. 1 (2009), 47–69.

26. Darling-Hammond, *The Flat World and Education*; Dunleavy, "Delegating Mathematical Authority; Kelly, "The Black-White Gap in Mathematics Course Taking."

27. William Schmidt and Curtis McKnight, *Inequality for All: The Challenge of Unequal Opportunity in American Schools* (New York: Teachers College Press, 2015).

28. Cirecie West-Olatunji et al., "Exploring How School Counselors Position Low-Income African American Girls as Mathematics and Science Learners," *Professional School Counseling* 13, no. 3 (2010).

29. Nicole M. Joseph, Ashli-Ann Douglass, and Mariah Harmon, "'I Like to do More Hands-On Stuff than Just Worksheets': High School Black Girls' Stories of their Experiences in Urban Mathematics Classrooms" (under review).

30. Brittany N. Anderson, "See Me, See Us: Understanding the Intersections and Continued Marginalization of Adolescent Gifted Black Girls in US

Classrooms," *Gifted Child Today* 43, no. 2 (2020): 86–100; Kristina Henry Collins, Nicole M. Joseph, and Donna Y. Ford, "Missing in Action: Gifted Black Girls in Science, Technology, Engineering, and Mathematics," *Gifted Child Today* 43, no. 1 (2020): 55–63; Jemimah L. Young, Jamaal R. Young, and Donna Y. Ford, "Standing In the Gaps: Examining the Effects of Early Gifted Education on Black Girl Achievement in STEM," *Journal of Advanced Academics* 28, no. 4 (2017): 290–312.

31. "Mathematics College and Career Readiness Standards," ACT, http://www.act .org/content/act/en/college-and-career-readiness/standards/mathematics -standards.html; "Substituting ACT/SAT for Smarter Balance Test Is Not a Smart Idea," *Ed Source*, https://edsource.org/2018/substituting-sat-act-for-the -smarter-balanced-test-is-not-a-smart-idea/601775#:ffi:text=In%20contrast %2C%20the%20SAT%20and,the%20high%20and%20low%20ends.

32. "Mathematics College and Career Readiness Standards," ACT; "Substituting ACT/SAT for Smarter Balance Test Is Not a Smart Idea," *Ed Source*.

33. "Mathematics College and Career Standards," ACT, https://www.act.org /content/act/en/college-and-career-readiness/standards/mathematics -standards.html.

34. Alex Heimbach, "Do You Need to Take the ACT for Community College?," *PrepScholar*, https://blog.prepscholar.com/do-you-need-to-take-the-act-for -community-college.

35. Heimbach, "Do You Need to Take the ACT for Community College?"

36. "Can My ACT Score Get Me A Scholarship?," UNIGO, https://www.unigo .com/scholarships/merit-based/act-scholarships.

37. Paul Black and Dylan Wiliam, "Assessment and Classroom Learning," *Assessment in Education: Principles, Policy & Practice* 5, no. 1 (1998): 7–74.

38. Black and Wiliam, "Assessment and Classroom Learning."

39. Neal Kingston and Brooke Nash, "Formative Assessment: A Meta-Analysis and a Call for Research," *Educational Measurement: Issues and Practice* 30, no. 4 (2011): 28–37.

40. Benjamin Bloom, "Learning for Mastery. Instruction and Curriculum," Regional Education Laboratory for the Carolinas and Virginia, *Topical Papers and Reprints* 1, no. 2 (1968): 1–11.

41. Linda C. Tilman, "Preface," in *The Sage Handbook of African American Education*, ed. Linda C. Tillman (Thousand Oaks, CA: Sage Press, 2007), ix.

42. "Principles and Standards," National Council of Teachers of Mathematics, https://www.nctm.org/Standards-and-Positions/Principles-and-Standards /?gclid=CjwKCAjwkN6EBhBNEiwADVfyaytNBK_Ia2asTRGIZqUpqzXrl 9zf1UNWX8d-FTrahtXwB3QFojar2xoCS4EQAvD_BwE.

43. Troy Hicks, "Make It Count: Providing Feedback as Formative Assessment," *Edutopia*, October 14, 2014.

44. Regula Grob, Monika Holmeier, and Peter Labudde, "Formative Assessment to Support Students' Competences in Inquiry-Based Science Education," *Interdisciplinary Journal of Problem-Based Learning* 11, no. 2 (2017): 6.

45. Neil Vigdor and Johnny Diaz, "More Colleges Are Waiving SAT and ACT Requirements," *New York Times*, May 21, 2020, https://www.nytimes.com/article/sat-act-test-optional-colleges-coronavirus.html?auth=link-dismiss-google1tap.

46. Vigdor and Diaz, "More Colleges Are Waiving SAT and ACT Requirements."

47. John Hattie and Helen Timperley, "The Power of Feedback," *Review of Educational Research* 77, no. 1 (2007): 81–112.

CHAPTER 6

1. Yolanda A. Johnson, "Come Home, Then: Two Eighth-Grade Black Female Students' Reflections on Their Mathematics Experiences," in *Mathematics Teaching, Learning, and Liberation in the Lives of Black Children*, ed. Danny Bernard Martin (New York: Routledge, 2009), 301.

2. Yasemin Copur-Gencturk et al., "Teachers' Bias Against the Mathematical Ability of Female, Black, and Hispanic students," *Educational Researcher* 49, no. 1 (2020): 30–43.

3. Copur-Gencturk et al., "Teachers' Bias Against the Mathematical Ability," 30.

4. Copur-Gencturk et al., "Teachers' Bias Against the Mathematical Ability," 37.

5. Copur-Gencturk et al., "Teachers' Bias Against the Mathematical Ability," 36.

6. Samantha D. Martin, "Invisible Girls: Victimization, Teacher Support, and Pathways to Punishment for Black Girls" (master's thesis, Georgia State University, 2019); Calvin Rashaud Zimmermann, "The Penalty of Being a Young Black Girl: Kindergarten Teachers' Perceptions of Children's Problem Behaviors and Student-Teacher Conflict by the Intersection of Race and Gender," *Journal of Negro Education* 87, no. 2 (2018): 154–68; Faiza M. Jamil, Ross A. Larsen, and Bridget K. Hamre, "Exploring Longitudinal Changes in Teacher Expectancy Effects on Children's Mathematics Achievement," *Journal for Research in Mathematics Education* 49, no. 1 (2018): 57–90.

7. Jemimah L. Young, Jamaal R. Young, and Robert M. Capraro, "Gazing Past the Gaps: A Growth-Based Assessment of the Mathematics Achievement of Black Girls," *Urban Review* 50, no. 1 (2018): 156–76; Nicole M. Joseph, Meseret F. Hailu, and Jamaal Sharif Matthews, "Normalizing Black Girls' Humanity in Mathematics Classrooms," *Harvard Educational Review* 89, no. 1 (2019): 132–55.

8. Zeus Leonardo, "The Color of Supremacy: Beyond the Discourse of White Privilege," *Educational Philosophy and Theory*, 36, no. 2 (2004).

9. Toya Jones Frank, "Teaching Our Kids: Unpacking an African-American Mathematics Teacher's Understanding of Mathematics Identity," *Journal for Multicultural Education* (2018); Toya Jones Frank, "Using Critical Race Theory to Unpack the Black Mathematics Teacher Pipeline," in *Critical Race Theory in Mathematics Education*, eds. Julius Davis and Christopher Jett (New York: Routledge, 2019), 98–122.

10. James Baldwin, "A Talk to Teachers," *Child Development and Learning* (1963): 7–12.

11. Baldwin, "A Talk to Teachers," 7.

12. Baldwin, "A Talk to Teachers," 7.

13. Rochelle Gutiérrez, "Strategies for Creative Insubordination in Mathematics Teaching," *Special Issue Mathematics Education: Through the Lens of Social Justice* 7, no. 1 (2016): 52–62; Juanita Ross Epp and Ailsa M. Watkinson, eds., *Systemic Violence in Education: Promise Broken* (New York: SUNY Press, 1997), 190.

14. Luis A. Leyva et al., "It Seems Like They Purposefully Try to Make as Many Kids Drop: An Analysis of Logics and Mechanisms of Racial-Gendered Inequality in Introductory Mathematics Instruction," *Journal of Higher Education* (2021): 1–31, doi: 10.1080/00221546.2021.1879586.

15. Baldwin, "A Talk to Teachers," 1.

16. Irene H. Yoon, "The Paradoxical Nature of Whiteness-At-Work in the Daily Life of Schools and Teacher Communities," *Race Ethnicity and Education* 15, no. 5 (2012): 587–613.

17. Yoon, "The Paradoxical Nature of Whiteness-At-Work," 597.

18. Yoon, "The Paradoxical Nature of Whiteness-At-Work," 608.

19. Soheyla Taie and Rebecca Goldring, "Characteristics of Public and Private Elementary and Secondary School Teachers in the United States: Results from the 2017–18 National Teacher and Principal Survey. First Look. NCES 2020-142," National Center for Education Statistics (2020).

20. Taie and Goldring, "Characteristics of Public and Private Elementary and Secondary School Teachers in the United States," 3.

21. Taie and Goldring, "Characteristics of Public and Private Elementary and Secondary School Teachers in the United States," 3.

22. "NTPS State Dashboard, 2017–2018: Georgia," National Center for Educational Statistics, https://nces.ed.gov/surveys/ntps/ntpsdashboard/Dashboard/GA.

23. "NTPS State Dashboard, 2017–2018: Louisiana," National Center for Educational Statistics, https://nces.ed.gov/surveys/ntps/ntpsdashboard/Dashboard/LA.

24. "NTPS State Dashboard, 2017–2018: Mississippi," National Center for Educational Statistics, https://nces.ed.gov/surveys/ntps/ntpsdashboard/Dashboard/MS;

25. NPTS State Dashboard, 2017–2018: District of Columbia," National Center |for Educational Statistics, https://nces.ed.gov/surveys/ntps/ntpsdashboard/Dashboard/DC; "NPTS State Dashboard, 2017–2018: Maryland," National Center for Educational Statistics, https://nces.ed.gov/surveys/ntps/ntpsdashboard/Dashboard/MD.

26. Alicia Davis and Greg Wiggan, "Black Education and the Great Migration," *Black History Bulletin* 81, no. 2 (2018): 12–16. https://doi.org/10.5323/blachistbull.81.2.0012.

27. Adam Fairclough, *A Class of Their Own: Black Teachers in the Segregated South* (Cambridge, MA: Harvard University Press, 2007).

28. "Race and Ethnicity of Public-School Teachers and Their Students: 2017," Institute of Education Statistics, https://nces.ed.gov/pubs2020/2020103.pdf.

29. "Digest of Education Statistics," National Center for Education Statistics, https://nces.ed.gov/programs/digest/d19/tables/dt19_209.10.asp.

30. "Race and Ethnicity of Public-School Teachers and Their Students: 2017," Institute of Education Statistics, https://nces.ed.gov/pubs2020/2020103.pdf.

31. "High School Mathematics Teachers: Demographics in the US," *Zippa, the Career Expert*, https://www.zippia.com/high-school-mathematics-teacher-jobs/demographics/.

32. Bisola Neil, "Using the 2011–12 Schools and Staffing Survey, Restricted File Version, to Identify Factors Associated with the Intent for African-American Math Teachers to Turnover" (diss., City University of New York, 2016), iv.

33. Neil, "Using the 2011–12 Schools and Staffing Survey," 243.

34. Danny B. Martin, "Teaching Other People's Children to Teach Other People's Children," in *Mathematics Teacher Education in the Public Interest: Equity and Social Justice*, eds. Laura J. Jacobsen, Jean Mistele, and Bharath Sriraman (Charlotte, NC: Information Age Publishing, 2012), 3–23.

35. "Robert Noyce Teacher Scholarship Program," National Science Foundation, https://www.nsf.gov/funding/pgm_summ.jsp?pims_id=5733; "Fellowships," Math for America, https://www.mathforamerica.org/fellowships; The Black Male Mathematics Teachers Project, https://www.mathteacherproject.org/collaborate.html.

36. "Are You a STEM Major Who Wants to Pursue a Teaching Career?," Peabody College of Vanderbilt University, https://peabody.vanderbilt.edu/admin-offices/stem-info-form.php.

37. National Center for Education Statistics, Integrated Postsecondary Education Data System, https://nces.ed.gov/ipeds/.

38. "63 Notable alumni of Fisk University," *EduRank*, https://edurank.org/uni/fisk-university/alumni/.

39. Heather J. Johnson, Teresa K. Dunleavy, and Nicole M. Joseph, "Noyce at Vanderbilt: Exploring the Factors That Shape the Recruitment and Retention of Black Teachers," in *Recruiting, Preparing, and Retaining STEM Teachers for a Global Generation*, eds. Jacqueline Leonard et al. (Boston: Brille Sense, 2019), 58–77.

40. Johnson et al., "Noyce at Vanderbilt," 63.

41. Johnson et al., "Noyce at Vanderbilt," 63.

42. Toya Jones Frank, "Using Critical Race Theory to Unpack the Black Mathematics Teacher Pipeline," in *Critical Race Theory in Mathematics Education*, eds. Julius Davis & Christopher Jett (New York: Routledge, 2019), 98–122, https://doi.org/10.4324/9781315121192-7.

43. Melinda A. Anderson, "A Root Cause of the Teacher Diversity Problem," *Atlantic*, https://www.theatlantic.com/education/archive/2018/01/a-root-cause-of-the-teacher-diversity-problem/551234/;Travis J. Bristol and Ramon B. Goings, "Exploring the Boundary-Heightening Experiences of Black Male Teachers: Lessons for Teacher Education Programs," *Journal of Teacher Education* 70, no. 1 (2019): 51–64; Micaela Y. Harris, "I'm That Nerd: Conceptualizing Black

Women Mathematics Teachers' Experiences That Lead to Their Retention" (under review).

44. Richard H. Milner and Tyrone C. Howard, "Black Teachers, Black Students, Black Communities, and Brown: Perspectives and Insights from Experts," *Journal of Negro Education* (2004), 285–97.

45. Cynthia CC DuBois and Diane Whitmore Schanzenbach, "The Effect of Court-Ordered Hiring Guidelines on Teacher Composition and Student Achievement," National Bureau of Economic Research, no. w24111 (2017).

46. DuBois and Schanzenbach, "The Effect of Court-Ordered Hiring Guidelines," 4.

47. DuBois and Schanzenbach, "The Effect of Court-Ordered Hiring Guidelines," 13.

48. DuBois and Schanzenbach, "The Effect of Court-Ordered Hiring Guidelines," 16.

49. Seth Gershenson et al., "The Long-Run Impacts of Same-Race Teachers," National Bureau of Economic Research, no. w25254 (2018).

50. Anna J. Egalite, Brian Kisida, and Marcus A. Winters, "Representation in the Classroom: The Effect of Own-Race Teachers on Student Achievement," *Economics of Education Review* 45 (2015): 44–52; Thomas S. Dee, "Teachers, Race, and Student Achievement in a Randomized Experiment," *Review of Economics and Statistics* 86, no. 1 (2004): 195–210.

51. Desire Carver-Thomas and Linda Darling-Hammond, "Why Black Women Teachers Leave and What Can Be Done About It," in *Black Female Teachers: Diversifying the United States' Teacher Workforce Advances in Race and Ethnicity in Education*, vol. 6, eds. Abiola Farinde-Wu and Ayana Allen-Handy (Bingley, UK: Emerald Publishing Limited, 2017), 159–84.

52. Toya Jones Frank et al., "Exploring Racialized Factors to Understand Why Black Mathematics Teachers Consider Leaving the Profession," *Educational Researcher* (2021): 0013189X21994498, 1.

53. My colleague Dr. Toya Jones Frank coined this phrase in a conversation we were having about how much of the mathematics education research is heady and theoretical, often forgetting that Black students will show up for class on Monday, so what can teachers do now. There is often a gap between theory and practice.

54. Francis Edward Su, "Mathematics for Human Flourishing," *American Mathematical Monthly* 124, no. 6 (2017): 483–93.

55. Danny B. Martin, "Teaching Other People's Children to Teach Other People's Children," in *Mathematics Teacher Education in the Public Interest: Equity and Social Justice*, eds. Laura J. Jacobsen, Jean Mistele, and Bharath Sriraman (Charlotte, NC: Information Age Publishing, 2012), 6.

56. William E. Cross Jr., "The Thomas and Cross Models of Psychological Nigrescence: A Review," *Journal of Black Psychology* 5, no. 1 (1978): 13–31; B. W. Jackson III, "Black Identity Development.," *New Perspectives on Racial Identity Development: Integrating Emerging Frameworks* 33 (2012).

57. Janet E. Helms, "Toward a Model of White Racial Identity Development," *College Student Development and Academic Life: Psychological, Intellectual, Social and Moral Issues*, eds. Philip G. Altbach, Karen Arnold, and Ilda Carreiro King (New York: Routledge, 1997): 49–66.

58. Bettina L. Love, *We Want to Do More Than Survive: Abolitionist Teaching and the Pursuit of Educational Freedom* (Boston: Beacon Press, 2019).

59. Robin DiAngelo, *White Fragility: Why it's so Hard for White People to Talk About Racism* (Boston: Beacon Press, 2018); Love, *We Want to do More Than Survive*.

60. Chayla M. Haynes and Lori D. Patton, "From Racial Resistance to Racial Consciousness: Engaging White STEM Faculty in Pedagogical Transformation," *Journal of Cases in Educational Leadership* 22, no. 2 (2019): 85–98.

61. Jenelle Reeves, "Teacher Investment in Learner Identity," *Teaching and Teacher Education* 25, no. 1 (2009): 34–41; Manka Varghese et al., "Theorizing Language Teacher Identity: Three Perspectives and Beyond," *Journal of Language, Identity, and Education* 4, no. 1 (2005): 21–44.

62. Jenelle Reeves, "Teacher Identity," in *The TESOL Encyclopedia of English Language Teaching*, 8 vols., ed. John I. Liontas (New York: Wiley-Blackwell, 2018), doi: 10.1002/9781118784235.eelt0268.

63. Julia Menard-Warwick, "The Cultural and Intercultural Identities of Transnational English Teachers: Two Case Studies from the Americas," *TESOL Quarterly* 42, no. 4 (2008): 617–40; Gloria Park, "I am Never Afraid of Being Recognized as an NNES: One Teacher's Journey in Claiming and Embracing her Nonnative-speaker Identity," *TESOL Quarterly* 46, no. 1 (2012): 127–51.

64. Aria S. Halliday, "Introduction: Starting from Somewhere Groundwork and Themes," in *The Black Girlhood Studies Collection*, ed. Aria S. Halliday (Toronto: Women's Press, 2019), 1.

65. Ruth Nicole Brown, *Hear our Truths: The Creative Potential of Black Girlhood* (Champaign: University of Illinois Press, 2013); Aimee Meredith Cox, *Shapeshifters: Black Girls and the Choreography of Citizenship* (Durham, NC: Duke University Press, 2015); Venus Evans-Winters, *Teaching Black Girls: Resiliency in Urban Classrooms*, vol. 279 (Boston: Peter Lang, 2005); Dominque Hill, "Blackgirl, One Word: Necessary Transgressions in the Name of Imagining Black Girlhood," *Cultural Studies↔Critical Methodologies* 19, no. 4 (2019): 275–83; Monique Morris, *Pushout: The Criminalization of Black Girls in Schools* (New York: The New Press, 2016); Lakisha Michelle Simmons, "Black Girls Coming of Age: Sexuality and Segregation in New Orleans, 1930–1954," (PhD dissertation, University of Michigan, 2009).

66. Brown, *Hear our Truths*, 1.

67. Nickolous Alexander Ortiz and Dalitso Ruwe, "Black English and Mathematics Education: A Critical Look at Culturally Sustaining Pedagogy," *Teachers College Record* 123, no. 10 (2021).

68. Deborah Loewenberg Ball, "Just Dreams and Imperatives: The Power of Teaching in the Struggle for Public Education," AERA 2018 Presidential Address, https://www.youtube.com/watch?v=JGzQ7O_SIYY.

69. Geneva Smitherman, "Black Language and the Education of Black Children: One Mo Once," *Black Scholar*, 27, no. 1 (1997): 28–35.

70. Nicole A. Bannister, "Reframing Practice: Teacher Learning Through Interactions in a Collaborative Group," *Journal of the Learning Sciences*, 24, no. 3 (2015): 347–72.

CONCLUSION

1. Paolo Freire, *Pedagogy of the Oppressed,* rev. (New York: Continuum, 1996).

2. Rochelle Gutiérrez, "Context Matters: How Should We Conceptualize Equity in Mathematics Education?," in *Equity in Discourse for Mathematics Education* (Dordrecht, Netherlands: Springer, 2012), 17–33.

3. Luis A. Leyva et al., "It Seems like They Purposefully Try to Make as Many Kids Drop: An Analysis of Logics and Mechanisms of Racial-Gendered Inequality in Introductory Mathematics Instruction," *Journal of Higher Education* (2021), 1–31; Brittany L. Marshall, Luis A. Leyva, and Taylor R. McNeill, "Instructors' and Students' Perceptions of Calculus Instruction Through the Lens of White, Patriarchal Benevolence" (Symposium paper presented in the annual meeting of the American Educational Research Association, Virtual conference, 2021).

4. Danny B. Martin, Paula Groves Price, and Roxanne Moore, "Refusing Systemic Violence Against Black Children: Toward a Black Liberatory Mathematics Education," in *Critical Race Theory in Mathematics Education* (New York: Routledge, 2019), 32–55; Django Paris, "Naming Beyond the White Settler Colonial Gaze in Educational Research," *International Journal of Qualitative Studies in Education* 32, no. 3 (2019): 217–24.

5. Nicole M. Joseph, Toya Jones Frank, and Taqiyyah Y. Elliott, "A call for a critical–historical framework in addressing the mathematical experiences of Black teachers and students," *Journal for Research in Mathematics Education* 52, no. 4 (2021): 476–90.

6. Toya Jones Frank, in-person conversation with author, October 21, 2016.

7. Nel Noddings, "The Caring Relation in Teaching," *Oxford Review of Education* 38, no. 6 (2012): 771–81.

8. Jane Swafford and Bradford Findell, *Adding It Up: Helping Children Learn Mathematics,* vol. 2101, ed. Jeremy Kilpatrick and National Research Council (Washington, DC: National Academy Press, 2001).

9. Marilee Ransom and Maryann Manning, "Teaching Strategies: Worksheets, Worksheets, Worksheets," *Childhood Education* 89, no. 3 (2013): 188–90.

10. Elli J. Theobald et al., "Active Learning Narrows Achievement Gaps for Underrepresented Students in Undergraduate Science, Technology, Engineering, and Math," *Proceedings of the National Academy of Sciences* 117, no. 12 (2020): 6, 476–83.

11. Elizabeth Fennema et al., "Increasing Women's Participation in Mathematics: An Intervention Study," *Journal for Research in Mathematics Education* 12, no. 1 (1981): 3–14.

12. Nicole M. Joseph, Ashli-Ann Douglas, and Mariah Harmon, "I Like to do More Hands-On Stuff than Just Worksheets," *High School Black Girls' Stories of their Experiences in Urban Mathematics Classrooms* (under review).

13. Bethany Rittle-Johnson, Jon R. Star, and Kelley Durkin, "How Can Cognitive-Science Research Help Improve Education? The Case of Comparing Multiple Strategies to Improve Mathematics Learning and Teaching," *Current Directions in Psychological Science* 29, no. 6 (2020): 599–609.

14. bell hooks, *Feminist Theory: From Margin to Center* (London: Pluto Press, 2000, original work published 1984).

15. hooks, *Feminist Theory*, 43.

16. Luis A. Leyva, "Black Women's Counter-stories of Resilience and Within-group Tensions in the White, Patriarchal Space of Mathematics Education," *Journal for Research in Mathematics Education* 52, no. 2 (2021): 117–51.

17. Leyva, "Black Women's Counter-stories of Resilience," 117.

18. Leyva, "Black Women's Counter-stories of Resilience," 139.

19. hooks, *Feminist Theory*, 43.

20. Adrienne D. Dixson, "'Let's Do This!' Black Women Teachers' Politics and Pedagogy," *Urban Education* 38, no. 2 (2003): 217–35.

21. Adrienne D. Dixson, "Democracy Now? Race, Education, and Black Self-determination," *Teachers College Record* 113, no. 4 (2011): 811–30; Monique Lane, "For Real Love: How Black Girls Benefit from a Politicized Ethic of Care," *International Journal of Educational Reform* 27, no. 3 (2018): 269–90; Bettina Love, *We Want to Do More Than Survive: Abolitionist Teaching and the Pursuit of Educational Freedom* (Boston: Beacon Press, 2019).

22. Toya Jones Frank et al., "Listening to and Learning with Black Teachers of Mathematics," *Rehumanizing Mathematics for Black, Indigenous, and Latinx Students* (Reston, VA: National Council of Teachers of Mathematics, 2018): 147–58.

23. Toya Jones Frank, Nicole M. Joseph, and Micaela Y. Harris, "Encyclopedia of Social Justice in Education," *Black Women Teaching Mathematics for Social Justice* (London: Bloomsbury, in press).

24. Frank et al., "Listening to and Learning with Black Teachers."

25. hooks, *Feminist Theory*, 63.

26. hooks, *Feminist Theory*, 65.

ACKNOWLEDGMENTS

I would like to acknowledge and thank my Harvard editor Jayne Fargnoli for her support in helping me to get this book completed. Dr. Richard Milner, the Race in Society series editor, believed in this project and mentored me through the process. I would also like to thank Dr. Toya Jones Frank, Dr. Ilana Horn, Dr. Teresa Dunleavy, Dr. Becky Peterson, Dr. Jackie Leonard, Dr. Crystal Morton, and Evan Taylor, who read drafts of the chapters and provided invaluable feedback. I also thank my Lord and Savior Jesus Christ for placing in me these dreams and desires to take up space examining Black girls and their mathematics experiences from a humanizing perspective. I bear witness to Black girls' radical possibilities of healing and liberation in mathematics contexts.

ABOUT THE AUTHOR

N ICOLE M. JOSEPH is an associate professor with tenure of mathematics education in the department of Teaching and Learning at Vanderbilt University. She is also the director of the Joseph Mathematics Education Research Lab (JMEL), which trains and mentors undergraduates, graduates, and postdoctoral students in Black Feminist and Intersectionality epistemological orientations producing theoretical and methodological practices that challenge hegemonic notions of objectivity to emphasize humanizing, empowering, and transformative research.

Dr. Joseph's research explores two lines of inquiry, (a) Black women and girls, their identity development, and their experiences in mathematics, and (b) gendered anti-Blackness, whiteness, and white supremacy and how these systems of oppression shape Black girls' and women's under-representation and retention in mathematics across the pipeline. Her scholarship has been published in top-tiered journals such as the *Journal of Negro Education, Harvard Education Review,* and *Teachers College Record.* Dr. Joseph's research perspective was also featured in *Essence Magazine* (February 2018), the premiere lifestyle, fashion, and beauty magazine for African American women with a readership of millions. Dr. Joseph's activist work includes founding the March for Black Women in STEM.

Dr. Joseph is also the lead faculty on a Trans-interdisciplinary Program Initiative (TIPs) grant called the Intersectional Experiences of Black Women and Girls in Society in collaboration with Vanderbilt faculty from Chemistry, Sociology, and the Divinity School. This grant includes five pillars of work including (1) the STEM Sistah Network, (2) mini research grants, (3) small group learning communities funding, (4) symposia, and (5) a summer research institute for middle school Black girls.

Dr. Joseph's most recent grant, Measuring Inclusive Constructs of Mathematics Identity (MICMI), provides timely information to educators on the intersecting identity created when race, gender, and disciplinary belonging converge—so that greater opportunities for learning and engagement are provided to preadolescent and adolescent girls. Co-design of the MICMI starts with Black girls as they identify the intersectional assets needed for more effective math learning that transcend a physical space or curriculum. The MICMI will provide actionable insights to educators, caregivers, and the girls themselves as they navigate the concurrent developmental trajectories associated with race, girlhood, and mathematics identities. MICMI is funded through Assessment for Good (AFG) and the Advanced Education Research & Development Fund (AERDF).

INDEX